Wild in the Kitchen

Also by Ronna Mogelon:

Famous People's Cats

.

Wild in the Kitchen

Recipes for Wild Fruits, Weeds, and Seeds

Ronna Mogelon

with illustrations by the author

M Evans

Lanham • New York • Boulder • Toronto • Plymouth, UK

M Evans
An imprint of Rowman & Littlefield
4501 Forbes Boulevard, Suite 200
Lanham, Maryland 20706
www.rowman.com

Library of Congress Cataloging-in-Publication Data

Mogelon, Ronna.
Wild in the kitchen : recipes for wild fruits, weeds, and seeds / Ronna Mogelon.
p.   cm.
Includes index.
ISBN 978-0-87131-946-3
1. Cookery (Wild foods) 2. Wild plants, Edible. I. Title
TX823 .M437 2001
641.6—dc21   2001023207

Distributed by
NATIONAL BOOK NETWORK

Typesetting by Evan Johnston

Printed in the United States of America.

Contents

Acknowledgments   9

Introduction   11

About Wild Edibles   12

About the Ingredients   13

Tips on Preserving and Canning   14

Berries
Barberries   18
Blackberries   20
Blueberries   23
Cloudberries and Partridgeberries   28
Currants and Gooseberries   30
Elder   33
Hawthorns   38
Nannyberries   40
Red and Black Raspberries   42
Strawberries   46

Flowers
Clover   54
Dandelions   56
Day Lilies   57
Elder Flowers   61
Sumac   62
Violets   64

In memory of Alex and Lila Mogelon, my dear parents—
supporters, tasters, and fans.

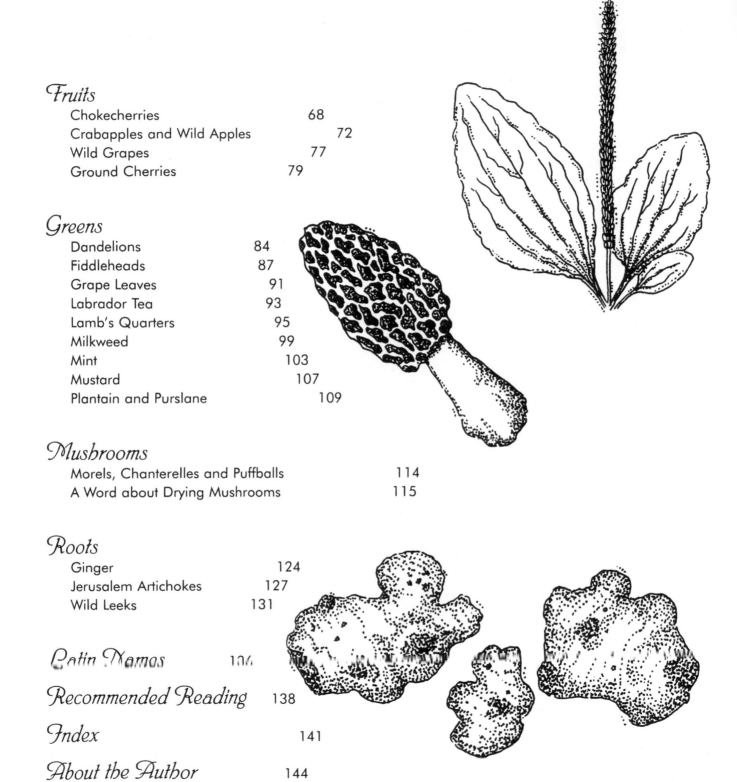

Fruits

Chokecherries 68
Crabapples and Wild Apples 72
Wild Grapes 77
Ground Cherries 79

Greens

Dandelions 84
Fiddleheads 87
Grape Leaves 91
Labrador Tea 93
Lamb's Quarters 95
Milkweed 99
Mint 103
Mustard 107
Plantain and Purslane 109

Mushrooms

Morels, Chanterelles and Puffballs 114
A Word about Drying Mushrooms 115

Roots

Ginger 124
Jerusalem Artichokes 127
Wild Leeks 131

Latin Names 134

Recommended Reading 138

Index 141

About the Author 144

Acknowledgments

Many people have helped me through various stages of this book. Special thanks to my parents, Lila and Alex, who suffered through strange smells coming out of the "test" kitchen. My mother passed away before this project came to fruition, but I can still hear her encouraging words. My father was probably my biggest fan—he tasted, tested, critiqued, and encouraged. He, too, passed away before this book was published. I dedicate this book to them.

Bob Graham's calls that he had located something else for my book were always exciting. He schlepped me here and there, always on the hunt for "one more thing" for the book. My sister, Marcia Mogelonsky, helped research, faxed me clippings and new ideas, and read and reread the manuscript. Peggi Calder answered all my e-mails, helped me sort through various wild edible confusions, proofread the manuscript, and went on wild-food forays into the countryside. Carol Downing at the Glengarry Bookstore helped me locate reference materials. And a big thank you to Peter Finney, who designed the cover.

Others helped in many ways. Thanks to all for tasting my experiments, lending or giving me books, picking me things from the backyard or the back forty, proofreading copy, and encouraging me, including: Barbara and Don Adeles, Amelia Ayre, Brigitte Beriault, Lynne Bowker, Bill and Dawn Bradford, Ken and Janet Brown, Francinna Collard, Frank and Anne Marie Collard, Rejean Duval, Sylvia Easdown, Nancy Flynn, Bill Gilsdorf, Herb and Sheba Goldstein, Jim and Janet Graham, Dodo and Norman Hecht, Susan Joiner, Judah and Wendy Katz, Brenda Kennedy, Norm Konlup, Barry and Kathy Lucking, Dieter and Astrid Meng, Larry and Maureen Mogelonsky, Claude Paquette, Yvon Paquette, Marlene Quesnel, Elisabeth Reboux, Al and Riva Regenstreif, Anne Schneider, Lis Skelly, Brian Smith, Steve Stober, Barry Strauss, Odile Têtu, Debbie Wightman, and Mac Williamson. Also thanks to Denis, Pauline, and Helen (the "Xerox Queen") at Alexandria Stationery.

I also want to thank two of my inspired and inspiring art teachers: Carole Irgo and Tib Beament. And my wonderful editor, PJ Dempsey, who made the whole experience a lot of fun.

And I can't forget my cats Domino, Cinnamon, and Nutmeg, who kept me company late at night while I was working on this book.

Author's Note

This book and its illustrations are not intended to be used as a field guide. Always take a good field guide with you when you are foraging for edibles. I recommend *A Field Guide to Edible Wild Plants: Eastern and Central North America* by Lee Allen Peterson, published by Houghton Mifflin, or *Edible Wild Plants: A North American Field Guide* by Thomas S. Elias and Peter A. Dykeman, published by Sterling.

Never guess at what you are picking. If you aren't 100 percent sure, *don't pick!* For safety's sake, do not taste or use any plant that you cannot positively identify.

The author and publisher are not responsible for any mistakes one might make in the field. Please be very, very careful.

Introduction

As a youngster, living in the suburbs of a large city, empty lots became my little bit of the natural world. I would spend hours picking wildflowers, pressing and drying them, identifying and faithfully recording them in my field guides. I saved my allowance for a pair of binoculars (which I still use) and was able to identify songbirds, which I spent a good deal of time drawing, determined to start my own field guide (entitled *Birds of Suburbia* perhaps?). My mother encouraged my love of nature by naming a daddy longlegs that had built its web outside our kitchen window. His name was Oscar, and we used to watch him catch his dinner as Mom cooked our own.

I distinctly remember running away from home. Like a hobo (which I thought was a moderately glamorous thing to be, at the time), I attached a red bandanna to a stick, filled it with peanut-butter-and-banana sandwiches, tied it up, and took off. I walked down our paved street, turned right, and headed for the local golf course, which was situated right beside the train tracks. The area beside the tracks was heavenly to me. Running for a good mile or so, it was completely wild and untouched—a conglomeration of old trees and stumps, wildflowers, toads and mice, running brooks, and tall grass. I used to get down on my belly in that long grass, completely hidden from the folks driving by for a day of golf. What a great secret I was, hidden in my secret garden.

That was the first place I discovered wild mint and milkweed with the help of my field guides, carried in my back pocket. Wild raspberries grew there, too, and it was exciting to pick some for dessert (after I finished the sandwiches, of course).

Eventually, I knew it was time to return. Strangely enough, I was back just in time to set the table for dinner. No one but me ever knew that I had run away from home.

Now, as an adult, there are days, after sitting at the computer or the drawing table for hours, when I feel like running back to those hidden woods. A more jaded hobo, but a hobo, nonetheless.

About Wild Edibles

Fiddleheads. Lamb's quarters. Morels. Dandelions. Many of these wild things are now appearing at your local greengrocer or supermarket. What can be done with them? This book will give you an inkling. It'll give you a chance to try something new.

It will also give you an idea of how to recognize these plants in the wild. Many of these weeds and fruits can be found in backyards and hedgerows. A Sunday drive in the country could prove fruitful as well. The illustrations and descriptions in this book will help you to discover when and where these plants are most easily found. If you decide to forage, be positive of what you are picking. There are some very good edible wild plant guides on the market, so be sure to take one along with you. A reliable field guide will help to assure you that what you are picking is really what you think you are picking! Don't guess! If you are in doubt, *don't take it home*.

As far as wild mushrooms go, proceed with caution. It is best to forage for mushrooms with an expert mycologist. I own many mushroom guide books and each one seems to have a different thing to say about most mushrooms. Fungi are rather elusive, and it is best to have several mushroom field guides to get a good handle on them. When I pick wild mushrooms, I am extremely careful and gather only four or five kinds that I am *absolutely* positive about. The rest I buy at the store.

In the back of this book is a list of the Latin names for all the plants mentioned. Wild things tend to go by various local names. Different places have different names for the same thing. Check the plant's Latin name and be sure of what you are getting.

There are literally hundreds upon hundreds of wild fruits, weeds, and seeds about which to write. I have chosen some of the easiest to recognize in the wild, also keeping in mind those that are available to city dwellers at the greengrocer. Most of the wild edibles described in this book are found in the northeastern United States and Canada. Many of them can be found nearly all over the continent.

The recipes in this book will enhance your cooking repertoire, whether you are a novice or an experienced cook. This is not a survival guide by any means. I tried to be inventive and have fun. That is really what this book is all about—having fun. Give it a try. Go wild in the kitchen!

About the Ingredients

Some general notes about the ingredients used in recipes for this book:

Butter: Use regular, salted butter. If you use unsalted butter, adjust the salt accordingly.

Citrus: Look for plump, heavy fruit when choosing oranges, lemons, or limes. These will be the juiciest. When using the citrus fruits for zest, be sure to wash the fruit very well, to remove any pesticides that might have been used on them. Buy a lemon zester or use a sharp paring knife, making sure to remove only the zest and none of the bitter, white pith underneath. If you end up with more zest than called for in the recipe, freeze it in plastic wrap for use another time.

Eggs: The eggs used in the recipes are large.

Flour: Use unbleached, all-purpose flour, unless otherwise specified.

Herbs: I prefer to use fresh herbs where possible as they have the best flavor. If these are unavailable, the general rule of thumb is to substitute one teaspoon of dried, crumbled herbs for one tablespoon of fresh, chopped herbs. If the dried herbs are finely ground, only use ¼ teaspoon. But taste your food as you add herbs, and use quantities that taste right to you.

Milk: It is your choice whether to use whole or low-fat milk. Obviously, a dish will taste richer if you use whole milk. (I prefer it in recipes but will use low fat-milk when I have guests who are watching their waistlines.) Nonfat milk makes the dishes watery, so I avoid using it.

Nuts: It is best to store nuts in the freezer, as their high fat content can make them go rancid quickly. That way, you can have a good variety at your disposal, and they won't go bad. Nuts taste better when toasted, and can be toasted directly from the freezer. Just lay them on a cookie sheet or toaster oven tray and bake them at 325°F for about 10 minutes, stirring them often, until they turn light brown and have a lovely aroma. Watch them carefully as they can burn very easily. Set aside to cool and use in any recipe calling for nuts.

Sugar: The sugar used most often in these recipes is white granulated sugar, unless otherwise specified.

Tips on Preserving and Canning

Some of the recipes in this book require a basic knowledge of preserving and canning. Use standard mason or canning jars with screw bands and lids, available at most grocery or hardware stores.

- Make sure that your jars don't have any cracks or nicks and that your lids are new. Don't reuse lids, as the rubber won't seal properly.

- Wash jars, lids, and screw bands in hot, soapy water, rinsing them well.

- To sterilize jars, boil them for at least 15 minutes in a large canner, fitted with a rack. (A canner is a large, deep pot that has a tight-fitting lid and a rack at the bottom.) If you don't have a canner, tie some screw bands together (the circles that hold the lids) and place them in the bottom of the pot to form a rack. Place the jars on top of the rack and fill the pot with enough water to cover the jars completely. Leave jars in the hot water until ready to fill.

- Before using the lids, boil them in water for 5 minutes, to soften and sterilize the sealing compound.

- When you are ready, ladle the prepared food into the hot jars, leaving about half an inch between the food and the rim. Adjust headspace as needed. This will enable the jars to seal properly. If necessary, wipe the rims of the jars to remove any stickiness. Place lids on jars and tighten screw bands until they are fingertip tight—not so tight that you can't reopen with more than just your fingertips (this allows some give between the jar and the lid).

- From a safety standpoint, it is wise to process anything you preserve in a boiling water canner. Once the fruit or pickles have been ladled into jars, replace the sealed jars into the boiling canner (making sure that the water covers the jars by at least one inch), cover, and boil half-pint or pint jars for 5 minutes. Larger jars require 10 minutes of boiling. (If you are at a higher altitude, you will have to process everything longer. Check a canning guide for the increased time ratio.) Generally, jams, jellies, and pickles high in vinegar, packed hot in half-pint or pint jars, need 5 minutes of boiling. Chutneys packed hot need 10 minutes. Make sure the canner has returned to a boil before starting the timer.

- Remove the jars and let them cool for 24 hours on a folded towel. As they cool, the lids snap down, creating an airtight seal. Make sure that the sealed lids curve downward. If this doesn't happen, the jar is not sealed properly and cannot be stored. Refrigerate these jars and eat the contents before those that have sealed properly. Or store canned jam, jellies, or chutneys in the refrigerator for up to 3 months.

- Do not eat (or even taste) discolored or spoiled-looking or funny-smelling food after it has been stored. Throw it away.

- Paraffin wax for sealing is no longer recommended, as it may contract and pull away from the sides of the jar.

Before doing any canning, it is highly recommended that you read the Ball Blue Book Guide to Home Canning, Freezing and Dehydration. *It is available on the Web site www.homecanning.com.* The Bernardin Guide to Home Preserving *is recommended for Canadian use and is available on the same Web site. These books and the site will help you with any detailed queries you may have about home canning.*

Gel Testing

There are some jam and jelly recipes in this book that refer to the gel test. The following list describes three ways to tell when your preserved food is ready.

- Using a candy thermometer is perhaps the easiest way to test for gelling. Cook the recipe to a temperature of 220°F (which is 8°F above boiling water). Your recipe will gel once this temperature has been reached.

- Another method is to put a saucer or plate in the freezer for 5 minutes. Take a small amount of your cooked recipe and drizzle a line of it across the frozen plate. It is gelled if you draw a spoon or finger across the line and it does not run back together.

- A third method is the spoon test, but it works only for jelly. Put a spoon in the freezer for 5 minutes, then dip it in the boiling jelly. Let the mixture run off the long side of the spoon. If it appears to sheet together (two drops run into each other and form one), then the jelly has set.

Types of Preserves

Different preserves have different names. Here are a few quick definitions:

- *Jam* is a mixture of fruit and sugar. The fruit is usually chopped or mashed.

- *Preserve* is about the same as jam, except that the fruit is in larger pieces.

- *Jelly* is clear and is made from sugar and cooked fruit that has been strained.

- *Marmalade* is jam made from citrus fruits (including the peel) and other added fruits.

- *Conserve* is a jam with raisins, nuts, and spices.

- *Fruit butter* is a spread made by cooking fruit and sugar until it has been reduced to a thick consistency.

- *Chutney* is a mixture of chopped fruit or vegetables seasoned with spices, vinegar, and sugar, making it a sweet-and-sour accompaniment to meats or cheeses.

Berries

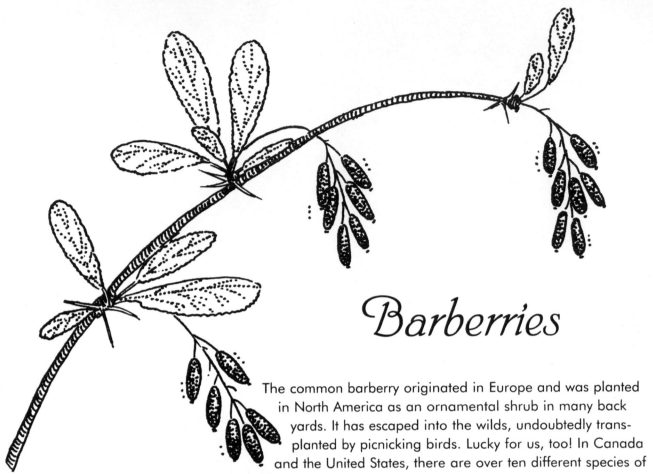

Barberries

The common barberry originated in Europe and was planted in North America as an ornamental shrub in many back yards. It has escaped into the wilds, undoubtedly transplanted by picnicking birds. Lucky for us, too! In Canada and the United States, there are over ten different species of this plant, but the common barberry is the most prolific fruit bearer.

In the springtime, look along roadsides, fences, and fields for tall bushes bearing yellow flowers that droop in showy clusters. By fall, the elongated, scarlet berries are visible, hanging in bunches. At the base of each hanging cluster are some nasty, three-pronged spines. Be careful to avoid these when picking.

Because of barberries' high pectin content, jelly made with these berries needs no additional pectin. The tartness of the barberry makes its jelly or jam a perfect accompaniment to meat and savory dishes. Adding more sugar makes barberry jam an excellent filling for pastry shells. The sweet syrup works well drizzled over ice cream or a fruit cup.

The bright red color of the fruit is reminiscent of red currants, and although the fruit is much more tart than currants, barberries have been dubbed the "poor man's red currant."

Barberry Jelly or Sweet or Savory Syrup

3–4 cups barberries
water to cover
¾–1 cup sugar
juice of half a lemon
1 cup water (for syrup only)

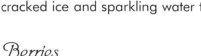

Rinse berries very well and pick out any leaves or large twigs (it is not necessary to strip fruit off stems). Place berries in a large pot, and add water to cover. Bring water to a boil and simmer until the fruit is soft, about 10 minutes. Put fruit and water through a food mill or sieve, pushing the fruit against the sieve with a wooden spoon to extract the pulp. The pulp and juice should measure about 1¼–1½ cups. Put them into a clean pot.

For jelly: add sugar and lemon juice and bring to a full rolling boil until gel stage has been reached (about 15 minutes). Pour into sterilized, hot jars, and seal immediately. Makes about a half pint (250 mL). Because the fruit has been pushed through a sieve, it will not be transparent like a regular jelly but more like a fruit butter or strained jam.

For syrup: add sugar, lemon juice, and 1 cup water. Bring to a boil for 10–15 minutes, until berry mixture starts to thicken a bit and looks syrupy. Check sweetness. Pour prepared syrup into sterilized bottles and seal. Process in a hot water bath (see pages 14–15 for instructions). Makes about two half pint (250 mL) jars.

Use syrup to baste a roast, or pour syrup over a just-out-of-the-oven round of Brie and serve warm with crackers. For a sweeter syrup to pour onto pancakes or fruit, you might want to add more sugar. Add a few spoonfuls of this syrup to a glass of cracked ice and sparkling water to create an unusual, refreshing drink.

Blackberries

These berries are sometimes confused with black raspberries, but there is definitely a difference. First of all, blackberries are downright huge! They are about two to three times larger than black raspberries. Another way to tell blackberries from black raspberries is that when you pick them, the little cores stay attached. (Black raspberries are hollow.)

Blackberries ripen from mid- to late summer (about a month later than black raspberries). And blackberries grow in moist areas, on very large canes—some can grow up to 8 feet tall, so you'll be on tiptoe picking them.

Blackberries can be used for pies or jam, just like any member of the raspberry family. But why not take advantage of their size? Try dehydrating them (either in a 200°F oven overnight, or in a dehydrator), and then store them in an airtight jar. You can add them to your morning granola. Or treat yourself to a midwinter pick-me-up by adding rehydrated blackberries to a fruit cup and tasting summer all over again.

Tipsy Blackberries

This is a wonderful Christmas gift. Start the process in late summer when the blackberries are ripe, and let them mellow through fall and into winter.

4–6 cups blackberries
1 cup sugar
light rum to cover

Wash the blackberries, picking over and discarding any stems or twigs. Mix the fruit with sugar in a bowl and set aside until the sugar starts to dissolve, about half an hour. Then place the sugared fruit into a large jar with a lid. Pour light rum over the fruit until the liquor covers all the berries. Place the jar in a cool, dark cupboard. Every week or two, give the jar a good shake. Your tipsy blackberries will be ready in about 3 months. Serve over vanilla ice cream, or slide a few berries onto a toothpick and serve with a cocktail.

To give as gifts, decant into smaller jars and reseal. Enjoy! Needs no refrigeration, and will last a few months in a dark, cool cupboard.

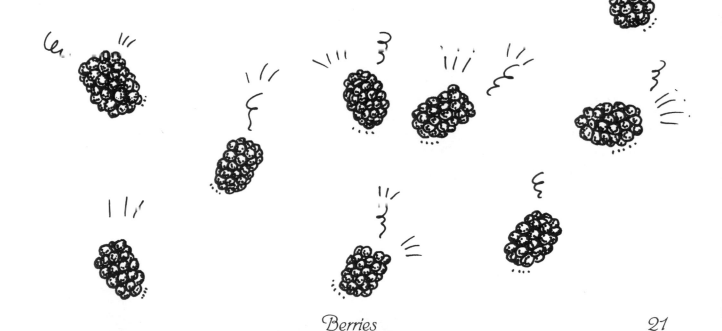

Blackberry Crisp

A very quick and easy dessert to throw together. You'll love the results.

Filling:
   3–4 cups blackberries, cleaned
   1 cup sugar (or more, depending
      on your taste)
   2 tablespoons cornstarch
   zest of an orange

Topping:
   ½ cup flour
   4 tablespoons brown sugar
   ⅓ cup butter
   ½ cup sliced almonds

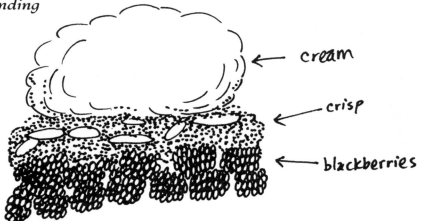

cream

crisp

blackberries

Place blackberries in the bottom of an ungreased, 8-inch square baking pan. Mix together the sugar, cornstarch, and orange zest and sprinkle on top of fruit. Set aside.

In a medium bowl, mix the flour and sugar together. Cut the butter in until the mixture is crumbly. Stir in almonds and pour over top of berries. Bake at 375°F for 35–40 minutes until the topping is crisp and golden brown. Serve warm with whipped cream or ice cream. Makes 4 to 6 servings.

Variations:
Almost any fruit can be added to this blackberry crisp. Throw in a few wild red raspberries to add a bit of color. If you have a few wild apples on hand, peel and slice them and stir them into the blackberries (add a few shakes of ground cinnamon, too).

Wild Blueberries

There are many species of wild blueberry, all with various names. Other names for blueberry include "bilberry," "whortleberry," and "deerberry" or "huckleberry." The huckleberry, which is a different genus altogether, tastes similar to the blueberry and can be substituted in recipes calling for blueberries. All are members of the heather family.

Blueberries and their kin grow in all sorts of places, from peat bogs to burned-out areas. In the spring, blueberry shrubs (which can be very short or up to 6 feet tall) bloom with white or pink bell-like flowers. By summer the berries are blue or almost black and ready to pick. They are delicious raw or cooked into jam, jelly, or pies.

If you are berry picking in bear country, beware! Black bears are especially fond of blueberries and are eager to get a mouthful. Go with a buddy and sing and talk loudly while you pick, to let the bears know you are there.

Wild Blueberry Squares

Filling:
- 4 cups wild blueberries
- juice and zest of 1 lemon
- ⅔ cup brown sugar
- ⅓ cup white sugar
- 4 teaspoons cornstarch
- 1 tablespoon butter

Base:
- 1 cup butter, softened
- 1 cup sugar
- 1 egg
- 2½ cups flour
- 2 teaspoons baking powder
- ¾ teaspoon salt

To make filling: In a medium saucepan, combine the blueberries and the juice and zest of the lemon. Cook over medium heat (uncovered) and stir until the berries start to soften and the mixture bubbles, about 6–8 minutes. Set aside.

Meanwhile, in a small bowl, stir together the brown sugar, white sugar, and cornstarch. Pour this mixture into the warm blueberries. Then stir in the butter. Let cool.

For the base: Beat butter, sugar, and egg until well mixed. In another bowl, combine the dry ingredients. Add wet to dry with a wooden spoon (mixture will be crumbly). Press two-thirds of the mixture into a lightly greased 9 × 13-inch pan. Stir the warm berry filling and spread it over the top of the base. Using your fingers or a fork, break up the remaining base mixture and sprinkle on top of the fruit. Do not press down. Bake at 350°F for 30 minutes. Cool and then cut into squares. Makes a lot of squares (depending on how you cut them!).

Wild in the Kitchen

Wild Blueberry Muffin Cake

This cake tastes just like a blueberry muffin . . . only it's a cake! Take it along on your next picnic or potluck dinner. It's sure to please a crowd.

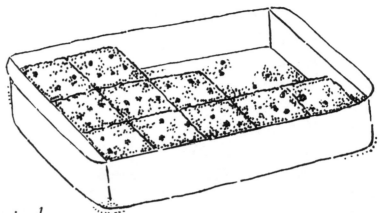

1 cup sugar
½ cup butter, melted
2 cups flour
2 teaspoons baking powder
2 eggs
milk (see below)
juice and zest of 1 lemon
1 cup wild blueberries
2 teaspoons cinnamon and sugar, mixed
2–3 tablespoons chopped walnuts (optional)

In a mixing bowl, beat the sugar and butter together until light. Add the flour and baking powder and mix well. Put 2 eggs in a cup measure and fill it to the top with milk. Add into the bowl, along with the lemon juice and zest, and beat well. Fold in 1 cup of wild blueberries until combined.

Pour the batter into a well-greased 9 × 13-inch pan. Sprinkle the top with the cinnamon and sugar mixture. Add walnuts if desired. Bake in a 350°F oven for 45–50 minutes (or until lightly browned and a pick inserted in the middle of the cake comes out clean). Let cool and serve right out of the pan. Makes 10–12 servings.

Wild Blue Yonder Pudding

3 cups fresh or frozen wild blueberries
⅓ cup water
1 teaspoon unflavored gelatin
¼ cup boiling water
½ cup sugar
2 teaspoons lemon juice
½ teaspoon cinnamon (optional)
loaf of sliced white or cinnamon bread
½ cup butter, melted
1 cup whipped cream, for garnish

If using fresh wild blueberries, put them in a saucepan with water and cook on medium heat until they are soft, about 5 minutes. If using frozen wild blueberries, thaw in the microwave on defrost for 5–10 minutes (they make their own juice, so no addition of water is necessary). Put blueberries and juice in a large mixing bowl.

Into a heat-proof measuring cup, combine the boiling water and ¼ cup of blueberry juice from the bowl and sprinkle gelatin over it. Let it soften for 5 minutes. Then stir it into the bowl of blueberries. To this mixture, add the sugar, lemon juice, and cinnamon (if you are using white bread). Stir well and set aside.

Remove the crusts from 14 slices of bread (more might be necessary for layers). Brush both sides of each slice with melted butter.

Line the insides of a 5 × 9-inch loaf pan with plastic wrap, leaving extra hanging outside of the pan. Put the slices of bread on the bottom and around the sides of the pan, trimming excess away. Spoon half of the blueberry mixture and juice into the pan. Then top with more bread slices, fitting them securely. Spoon the remaining half of the blueberry mixture over that. Top that off with more bread. Press the sides into the bottom (it might be necessary to trim the sides if they are too long). Fold the plastic wrap over and seal very well. Press down on the loaf to make sure it is quite firm and will stick together.

Refrigerate overnight. When ready to serve, invert the loaf onto a cutting board and unwrap. Cut 1-inch slices, lay them flat on a plate, and add a dollop of whipped cream. Makes 9 servings.

Wild Blueberry Syrup

4 cups wild blueberries
⅓ cup water
sugar (see below)

Put the wild blueberries and water into a medium saucepan. Mash the berries and bring the mixture to a boil. Lower the heat and let simmer for an hour, stirring and mashing occasionally.

At this point, you can decide if you want a lumpy, fruity syrup or a refined, smooth syrup. If you want a lumpy, fruity syrup, add the sugar now. Add approximately 1½ cups sugar to 2 cups fruit mixture, but taste it before adding all the sugar. (You might like it tarter or sweeter.) Bring the fruit-and-sugar mixture to a boil, stirring until all the sugar has dissolved. Skim off any foam from the top and let boil for 5 minutes. Pour into bottles and seal. Store in the refrigerator for up to 3 months.

If you want a refined, smooth syrup, after cooking for an hour, strain the contents of the pot through a wet jelly bag and let drip (this might take an hour or two). Squeeze the bag to extract as much liquid as possible. Then filter the liquid through a cheesecloth.

Return the liquid to a clean pot and measure 1½ cups sugar for every 2 cups of juice. Bring the syrup to a boil and make sure to stir it well, until the sugar is dissolved. Skim off foam and let boil for 5 minutes. Pour into bottles and seal. Store in the refrigerator for up to 3 months. Makes about 3 cups. Choose decorative bottles and give as gifts.

wild blueberry syrup

Cloudberries and Partridgeberries

Both of these berries are found mainly in northern climes. Cloudberries are abundant in Newfoundland and Labrador, and are found as far south as Maine and New Hampshire. Partridgeberries grow in most of northeastern Canada and the United States.

Cloudberries, also known as bakeapples, look like golden raspberries, but their taste is remarkably unraspberrylike. This small, low plant grows on boggy ground and bears only a single fruit, which ripens in August.

Cloudberries can be served just picked, topped with a bit of sugar and cream. Or they can be made into delicious jams and pies. For a wonderful dessert, try the liqueur called Lakka (distilled in Finland from cloudberries) over vanilla ice cream, topped with a handful of fresh cloudberries.

Similar in flavor to cranberries, partridgeberries are bright red when ripe but look like blueberries when cooked. The plant is a creeping stem, which at its end produces two white or pink flowers. It grows in moist woods and blooms in June or July. Partridgeberries can be picked from July through to winter. Partridgeberries are not overly sweet and can be made into pie fillings, jams, and the like. Or they can be tossed into salads raw.

cloudberry

partridgeberries

Partridgeberry jam is easy to make. Measure whatever amount of berries you have and add them to a saucepan along with a small amount of water (to keep the berries from burning). Add half as much sugar (or a bit more for a sweeter jam) as you have berries, along with the juice and the zest of a lemon. Simmer for 15–20 minutes and seal in hot, sterile jars. Process in a hot water bath (see pages 14–15 for instructions).

Cloudberry Muffins

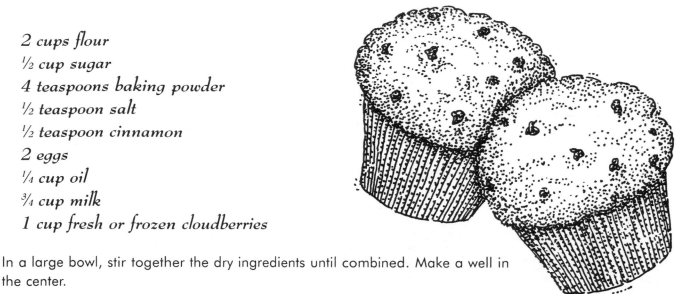

2 cups flour
½ cup sugar
4 teaspoons baking powder
½ teaspoon salt
½ teaspoon cinnamon
2 eggs
¼ cup oil
¾ cup milk
1 cup fresh or frozen cloudberries

In a large bowl, stir together the dry ingredients until combined. Make a well in the center.

In a separate bowl, beat eggs until light in color. Add oil and milk, beat again, and then stir in the cloudberries. Add wet ingredients to dry and stir only until moistened (do not overmix); the batter will be lumpy. Fill greased muffin tins or put batter in a muffin pan lined with paper cups. Bake for 20–25 minutes (or until golden brown) in a 400°F oven. Makes 12–18 big muffins.

Currants and Gooseberries

These two plants are from the same genus and have very similar characteristics. Both have maplelike leaves and grow on small, sprawling bushes. Look for them along old fences, in hedgerows, or in the woods in midsummer when they start to bear fruit.

currants

When ripe, currants can be red, golden, or purple-black. They are small but grow in multiple hanging clusters, so they can be gathered fairly easily. Many currants can be eaten raw, but some species are rather tart, so are better made into jams, jellies, or pies.

Gooseberries, when ripe, can be pale green, reddish, pink, or purple. They grow singly or in small clusters, with long tails coming from their ends. Most wild gooseberries feel like tiny, round porcupines! They are barbed and very difficult to pick. The prickles can make a day of picking very trying, even if you wear leather gloves. You might be lucky enough to find a plant without the barbs. Pick these and enjoy! If not, you can still make jelly with spiny gooseberries, but be sure to strain them through a food mill or sieve and then through cheesecloth to remove any trace of prickles. And be generous with the sugar. Gooseberries, whether smooth or bristly, are very tart.

gooseberries

Hint 1: As currants don't all ripen at the same time, I usually pick as many ripe currants as I can find, and put my cache into an airtight container in the freezer. Every week for 4–5 weeks (as more and more currants ripen), I pick the fruit and add them to the others. Eventually I have enough collected for a pie or two or for lots of delicious jelly.

Hint 2: If you are picking fruit for jelly, make sure to add a few unripe ones into your basket—they are full of pectin and will help ensure that your jelly sets.

Wild in the Kitchen

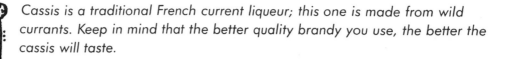

Wild Cassis

Cassis is a traditional French current liqueur; this one is made from wild currants. Keep in mind that the better quality brandy you use, the better the cassis will taste.

2 cups wild black currants
1 cup brandy
1–2 cups sugar

Wash the currants well and put them into a quart jar. Pour the brandy over them (the brandy should cover the currants) and seal the jar tightly. Leave it in a dark cupboard for 2 months. Give the jar a shake every week or so.

When 2 months have passed, pour the juice and fruit into a cheesecloth or jelly bag. Let it drip into a bowl. When it has stopped dripping, squeeze out any remaining liquid. To make sure the liquid is extremely clear, discard the old cheesecloth and run the liquid through 2 layers of fresh cheesecloth. Return the liquid to the jar.

Add sugar to taste, and reseal the jar. Leave it in a dark cupboard for another 2 weeks. At that point, the sugar should all have dissolved and the dark liquid should have turned clear. (It it hasn't, filter it again.) Decant the liquid into smaller sterilized jars, then seal. Yields 1 cup.

Wild Cassis Cocktails

Wild Cassis Bubbly Cocktail

You can make a bubbly cocktail with your wild cassis. Fill a highball glass halfway with seltzer, club soda, or sparkling water. Add cracked ice and top it off with wild cassis.

Kir

Add 2 teaspoons of wild cassis to a glass of white wine.

Kir Royale

Add 2 teaspoons of wild cassis to a glass of Champagne.

Ballet Russe Cocktail

To make this 1940s drink, combine 2 oz. vodka, ½ oz. wild cassis, and 3 teaspoons lime juice in a cocktail shaker. Shake and serve in a cocktail glass. Garnish with a slice of lime.

Pompier Highball or Vermouth Cassis

Into a highball glass, pour 3 oz. vermouth, 3–4 tablespoons wild cassis, and a shot of seltzer, club soda, or sparkling water. Stir to combine. Top it off with a curl of lemon peel.

Elder

The elder shrub has had multiple uses since pioneer days. The flowers can be added to pancakes or dipped in batter and deep-fried to make delicious fritters. There are myriad recipes for the berries, ranging from the popular elderberry wine to syrups, custards, pies, chutneys, and more.

The berries grow from a single root to a height of 3 to 10 (or more) feet. Broad white flowers (about 4 to 6 inches in diameter) grow in umbrellalike clusters preceding the purple or black berries; these will help you locate the bushes early for late summer picking. You'll find elderberries everywhere, along country roads or pathways, and around old fences and barns. When the berries mature, many times they weigh down the branches . . . and you'll have competition from the birds for this delicious treat.

Avoid the red-fruited elder as it is bitter and somewhat toxic.

Hint: There are many suggestions for the best way to strip elderberries off their stems. Some people use a fork, with varying degrees of success. Others try freezing the stems and berries on cookie sheets, reasoning that the berries are less likely to be crushed when pulled off their stems because they are frozen (and that they'll detach easier). I try to nudge the just-picked berries off their stems by rubbing them gently between my fingers. Don't coax them too hard or you'll crush them!

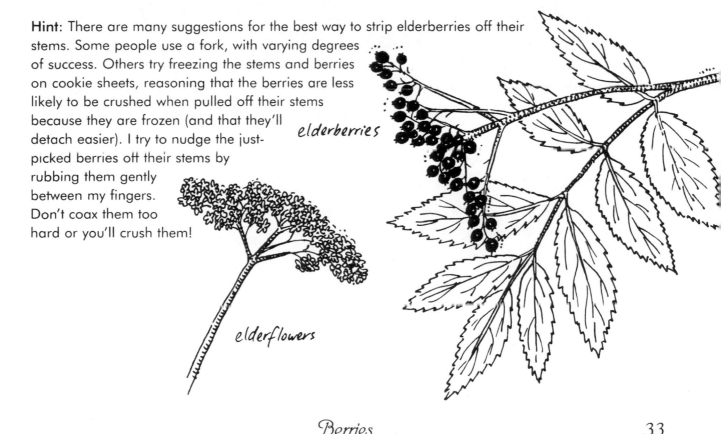

elderberries

elderflowers

Elderberry Triangles

These little pastries have an interesting flavor and their texture is slightly crunchy (similar to that of a fig), due to the tiny seeds of the elderberry.

Pastry:
  2 cups all-purpose flour
  ¾ teaspoon salt
  ½ cup shortening
  ½ cup butter
  3 tablespoons cold water

Filling:
  1 cup elderberries
  4 tablespoons honey
  1 teaspoon cinnamon
  ½ teaspoon nutmeg

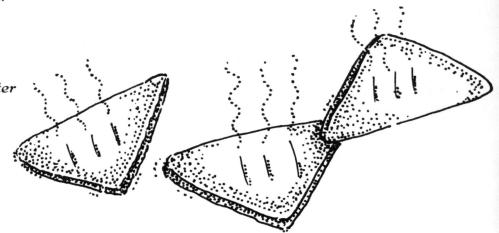

Mix flour and salt together. Cut the shortening and butter into the flour mixture with a pastry blender until the crumbs look uniform, or roughly like oatmeal. Sprinkle the cold water over the mixture and stir until moistened. Try not to overwork pastry as it will lose its flakiness and become tough. Wrap in waxed paper or plastic wrap and let rest in the refrigerator for at least 15 minutes.

Remove the elderberries from their stems and rinse clean. Pick over and discard any dried berries or stem ends. Mix with the honey, cinnamon, and nutmeg. Set aside.

Divide dough in half (it is easier to work with a smaller amount). Roll dough onto a floured surface and cut into squares about 5 × 5-inch. Put about a teaspoon of the fruit mixture in one corner of the square. Moisten the opposite corner of the square with water (the water acts like glue) and fold over, sticking the sides together to make a triangle. Press sides together tightly so no juice escapes while baking.

Place on an ungreased baking sheet. Make 2 or 3 slits in the top of each triangle to let steam escape. Brush with milk and sprinkle with sugar. Bake for 25 minutes, at 400°F (or until golden brown). Makes about 15–20 little pastries.

Wild in the Kitchen

Elderberry Marmalade

If you don't like spending a lot of time picking elderberries off their tiny stems, this is the recipe for you because all of the ingredients are strained.

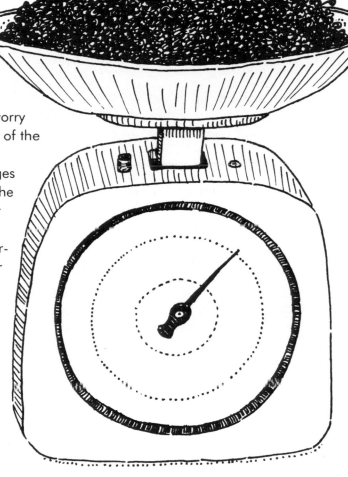

12–14 apples
1–2 cups water
1–1½ lbs. (1 quart or 4 cups) elderberries
2 limes
3 oranges
5 cups of sugar

Wash and quarter apples (don't bother peeling or coring) and add them to a large pot with about an inch or two of water on the bottom. Cook until apples get mushy. Add rinsed elderberries (don't worry too much about removing the stems) and the juice of the limes and oranges. Make sure the pits have been removed, and put the rinds of the limes and oranges into a food processor and grind them up. Add to the fruit mixture. Then stir in 5 cups of sugar. Cook for about an hour, or until set. Strain the mixture through a food mill or sieve and pour into hot, sterilized jars. Seal immediately. Process in a hot water bath (see pages 14–15 for instructions).
Makes 5–6 half-pint (250 mL) jars.

Elderberry Wine

Although the name "wine" implies a fermented drink, this is more of a liqueur. Old-timers called it elderberry wine and somehow the term has stuck.

> *elderberries (4 or more cups)*
> *gin or brandy to cover*
> *1 cup sugar*
> *2 cups water*

Wash whatever amount of berries you have (4 cups will do) and put them in a quart (or liter) jar. Cover the berries with gin or brandy. Seal and let stand in a dark cupboard for one month. Filter juice through a cheesecloth or paper coffee filter. Set aside.

Make a sugar syrup (roughly 1 cup of sugar to 2 cups water) in a small saucepan. Heat through until the sugar dissolves completely. Cool and add to elderberry juice. Taste to make sure there is enough sugar.

Rebottle, seal, and store for another 2 to 3 months, shaking from time to time. Decant into smaller bottles, either for gifts or consuming. Needs no refrigeration.

Elderberry and Peach Cake

Elderberries are ripe in the field at the same time that peaches are ripe in the orchard (or the store). They make wonderful bedfellows.

½ cup butter, softened
½ cup sugar
zest of 1 orange
2 eggs
1 cup flour
1 teaspoon baking powder
¼ teaspoon salt
1½ cups peeled and sliced peaches (about 4
*   peaches)*
1 cup elderberries (stripped off their
*   stems, rinsed, and picked over)*
⅓ cup sugar
½ teaspoon cinnamon
¼ cup chopped walnuts

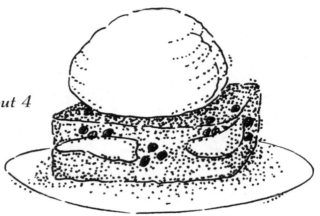

In an electric mixer, cream together the butter and sugar until light. Add the orange zest and eggs and beat well. Add flour, baking powder, and salt and mix until very well incorporated (the batter will be heavy and thick).

Spread a little more than half of the batter into a well-greased 9 × 9-inch pan. On top of the batter, spread the peaches and the elderberries. Drop remaining batter by spoonfuls on top (it will spread). Sprinkle the sugar, cinnamon, and walnuts on top.

Bake at 350°F for 50 minutes. Let cool for 15 minutes or so, and serve warm right out of the pan with whipped cream or ice cream. Serves 6–8.

Hawthorns

The hawthorn is a dense shrub or small, craggy tree that grows in rocky woods or old fields. In springtime, the branches bear five-petaled blooms that can be white or pale pink. By fall, the fruits have formed and are generally red when ripe (some may be orange, yellow, or nearly black). These applelike fruits called haws or hawberries are smaller than crabapples and resemble rose hips. Be careful, the crooked branches have very long, sharp thorns. The fruit can be wormy, so search around for pest-free hawberries.

The hawthorn is a genus of the rose family. There are some 26 edible species of hawthorns in North America . . . some drier or sweeter than others. Sample the berries to find the tastiest before picking a bucketful.

Even though the tiny fruits can be dry, they make a delicious jelly. And since the hawberries are full of pectin, you can almost be sure of making a jelly that sets. For an unusual-tasting tea, steep a few crushed haws with fresh wild mint in boiling water for a few minutes, strain and enjoy.

The berries can be used fresh or dried and can be substituted in recipes calling for rose hips. For use in winter, dry the haws in a 200°F oven and store in a cool, dark cupboard.

Interestingly, the hawberry is a fairly good source of vitamin C and is said to have helped the aboriginal people and first settlers of Manitoulin Island ward off scurvy. (Manitoulin Island is the largest freshwater island in the world, located in north central Ontario, Canada.) To this day, people born on Manitoulin Island are called "Haweaters."

Hawthorn Jelly

After you have extracted the juice from the hawberries, it looks rather muddy. As soon as you add the lemon juice, the color changes to a lovely pink.

7 cups hawberries
water (to cover)
½ cup fresh lemon juice (strained)
1 envelope powdered or liquid pectin
4 cups sugar

Rinse the hawberries well in water, removing any dirt (don't bother trimming ends or cutting them up). Put into large saucepan, add water to cover the fruit, and bring to a boil. Cover and simmer until soft (about half an hour). Crush them with a potato masher (or put in a blender). Then strain through a jelly bag or cheesecloth, squeezing the bag a bit. Measure 4 cups of liquid (add a bit more water through the jelly bag, if necessary) into a large pot. (Make sure not to add the small black bits that have settled to the bottom of the liquid.)

Set the pot over medium-high heat. Add strained lemon juice and bring to a boil. Add the pectin crystals and bring to a full, rolling boil. Then stir in the sugar, boil for another minute, and remove from the heat. Bottle in sterilized jars. Process in a hot water bath (see pages 14–15 for instructions). Makes 3 or 4 half-pint (250 mL) jars.

Nannyberries

Nannyberries grow on tall shrubs or small trees on rocky hillsides or at the edges of forests. In spring, they bear gorgeous, pompom flowers made up of tiny, white blossoms. (Because they are so pretty, many people have planted nannyberry bushes in their backyards as ornamentals.) By fall, the flowers have turned into bunches of oval berries that become purplish blue as the leaves change color. This is when they are sweetest and ready to be picked.

The nannyberry, along with some other fruits of the *Viburnum* species are also known as "wild raisins" because they eventually shrivel up and look like raisins. They stay hanging on their branches throughout most of the winter, which makes them a wonderful survival food.

Nannyberries taste somewhat like raisins and have the texture of dates or prunes. The fruit can be nibbled fresh while on the trail. Also the beries can be cooked in water and strained, to remove the berries' single, flat seeds, and combined with sugar to make a delicious spread.

Wild in the Kitchen

Spiced Nannyberry Butter

This spread looks like a rich, dark prune butter and tastes great on hot toast.

2–3 quarts of nannyberries
cold water to cover
¹/₂–³/₄ cup sugar (to taste)
¹/₂ teaspoon cinnamon
¹/₂ teaspoon ground cloves
¹/₄ teaspoon allspice
¹/₄ teaspoon nutmeg

Put washed nannyberries in a large saucepan and cover with cold water. Bring to a boil and let simmer for 30–40 minutes, until softened. Pour contents of pot into a food mill or sieve and press pulp through it. You should have about 2 cups of pulp. Return it to a clean pot and add sugar and spices. Cook until the mixture has thickened to a spreadable consistency, about 30–45 minutes. Put into hot, sterilized jars and seal immediately. Process in a hot water bath (see pages 14–15 for instructions). Makes 4–5 half-pint (250 mL) jars.

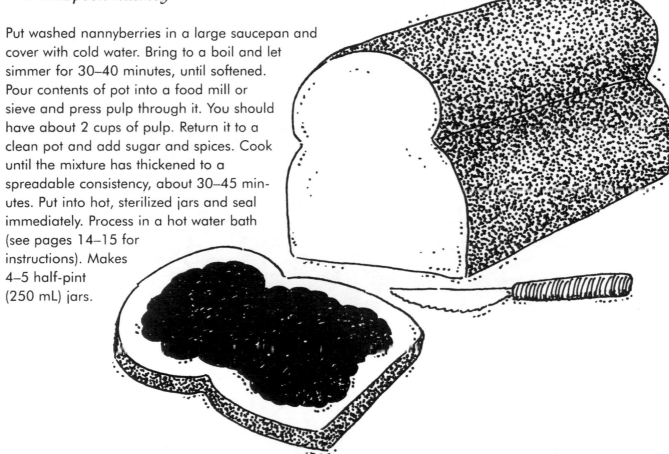

Wild Red and Black Raspberries

Red and black raspberries are members of the rose family, which means they are full of thorns, so it's best to cover your arms and legs when picking. Both of these berries ripen at about the same time (in midsummer), so if you are lucky, your basket will have a good combination of both red and black berries.

Black raspberries have canes that curve down to the ground. When the tips touch the ground, they set root . . . which is where they'll come up next year. So black raspberries change their locations slightly from year to year, depending on where they set their tips.

Wild red raspberries are smaller than their domestic cousins, but they are twice as tasty. You'll know when they are ripe—they are almost impossible to pull off their stem when they aren't. But don't tug too hard. Come back in a day or two, and they will be happy to come home with you.

Black raspberries are initially red, then turn purple when they are ready to be picked. They are firmer and less juicy than red raspberries, but chances are you'll still have purple fingertips when you're done picking.

Avoid washing the berries—they tend to get mushy when wet. To clean them, just check them over carefully, removing any leaves or critters.

black raspberries

wild red
raspberries

Wild in the Kitchen

Raspberry Pudding Cake

2 eggs
1 cup sugar
¾ cup milk
1 teaspoon vanilla
½ cup butter, melted
2 cups flour
2 teaspoons baking powder
pinch of salt
2 cups black and/or red
    raspberries
berries for garnish (optional)

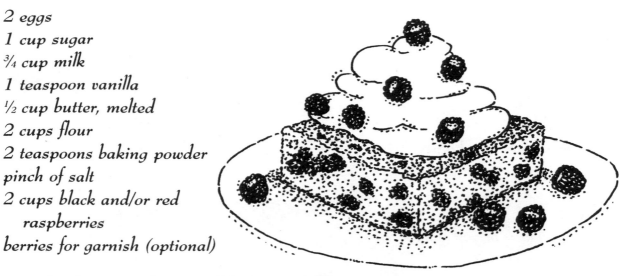

Beat together the eggs and sugar until frothy.
Add the milk and vanilla, then the melted butter
and beat well.

In a separate bowl, mix together the flour, baking powder, and salt.
Add the dry ingredients to the wet and beat until the batter is
smooth. Gently fold in the fruit.

Put the batter in a lightly greased 9 × 13-inch pan. Bake for 30 minutes in a
350°F oven, until lightly browned (or until a pick comes out clean). Serve
warm or at room temperature with a scoop of ice cream or whipped cream on top, and
garnish with a few reserved berries. Serves 8–10.

Raspberry Galette

Instead of worrying about a perfectly finished pie, why not try a free-form galette? It is a sort of "pie sculpture," usually oval, sometimes roundish. You decide what it will look like.

Pastry:
    1¼ cups all-purpose flour
    1 tablespoon sugar
    pinch of salt
    6 tablespoons cold butter
    2–3 tablespoons cold water

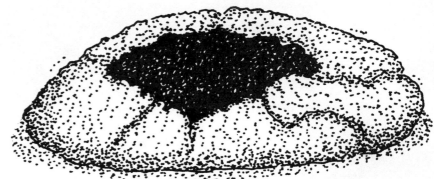

Filling:
    2 cups black or red raspberries
    5 teaspoons sugar
    2 tablespoons flour

To prepare the pastry, combine the flour, sugar, and salt in a bowl and mix well. Using a pastry blender or your fingers, break the butter up into pieces, until the mixture resembles coarse oatmeal. Sprinkle the water over the mixture; add only enough water that when stirred, the pastry forms a ball and holds together (this may depend on how humid it is outside). Knead the pastry a few times (don't overwork it), and wrap it in waxed paper or plastic wrap. Refrigerate the pastry for 30 minutes or so.

For the filling, mix cleaned berries with sugar and flour and stir well.

Roll out the chilled dough on a surface that has been lightly floured. Your finished flattened dough should be roughly 10 to 11 inches around. Place it on a foil-covered baking sheet. Put berry filling in the middle of the dough and fold up the sides of the pastry all around the filling, pressing it together. Don't try to cover all the fruit—leave about a 3-inch opening in the middle of the tart. If there are any holes or cracks on the sides of the galette, patch with a little excess pastry from the edge and use water as the glue (you don't want to spring any leaks). If you do spring a leak, fold up the sides of the aluminum foil, to create a sort of basin in which to catch your leaks.

Bake in a 350°F oven for 40–50 minutes, until the crust is golden. Serve warm or at room temperature. Makes enough for 6 people.

                                   Wild in the Kitchen

Raspberry Vinegar

Red raspberries make a dark red vinegar; black raspberry vinegar is purple-red.

3 cups white vinegar
1 cup black or red raspberries

In a saucepan, bring the vinegar to a boil for 2 minutes. Then set it aside to let cool a bit. Put the raspberries into a quart jar, then pour the warm vinegar on top. Seal the jar and place it in a sunny spot for 2 weeks. Shake the jar from time to time. Strain the vinegar through a cheesecloth, pour into sterilized jars, and seal. Makes nearly a quart. Can be used in salad dressings and vinaigrettes. Or splash over sweetened strawberries for dessert.

Marci's Raspberry Chicken

One of my sister's signature meals. It tastes wonderful served over plain rice.

1 tablespoon butter
4 half chicken breasts, boneless and skinless
1 large onion, minced finely
4 tablespoons raspberry vinegar
1 tablespoon tomato paste
¼ cup chicken broth or white wine

In a frying pan, melt the butter and add the chicken breasts, browning them on both sides. Remove the chicken from the pan and place on a tray. Cover with foil and keep warm in the oven.

Meanwhile, return the pan with the butter and chicken juices to the stove and add the minced onion. Cover the pan and sweat the onions over low heat for 15 minutes, or until the onions are limp (do not brown). Stir occasionally. Add the raspberry vinegar and turn the heat to high, boiling the vinegar until it has been reduced to a small puddle. Add the tomato paste and chicken broth or wine.

Remove chicken from the oven and return it to the frying pan. Turn the heat down to low and cook covered, until the chicken is cooked through, about 10–15 minutes. Put chicken on a serving platter and top it off with pan scrapings and whatever liquid is left in the pan. Garnish with fresh raspberries, if desired. Serves 4.

Wild Strawberries

In the springtime, you might notice the little three-leafed green plants, with their attractive white flowers. These are wild strawberries, waiting to do their stuff. By mid- to late June, they are ready to be picked and are delicious! But they are tiny and one must be a very patient forager to be able to pick them in large quantities. If you want to make a lot of jam, or a pile of pies, I suggest that you buy commercial strawberries. But if you want a wonderfully sweet and intense flavor, keep picking the wild ones and enjoy. The following recipes have kept in mind the fact that it might be a daunting task to collect, clean, and hull large amounts of wild strawberries. So the quantities of the wild strawberries have been kept to 2 cups or under.

Wild in the Kitchen

Wild Strawberry Sauce

1 cup wild strawberries, cleaned and hulled
½ cup sugar
juice and zest of 1 lemon

Mix all ingredients together in a saucepan. Mash the berries lightly with a wooden spoon. Heat through slowly and bring to a boil. Simmer for 5 minutes (don't add any liquid, as the strawberries are juicy when cooked). Let cool. Tastes great on vanilla ice cream or a stack of pancakes! Makes enough for one or two servings.

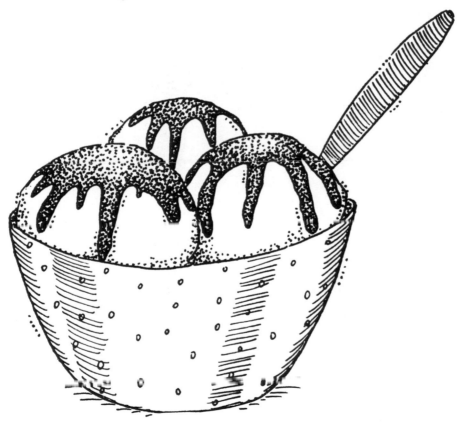

Wild Strawberry Smoothie

½ cup wild strawberries, cleaned and hulled
½ cup plain yogurt
½ cup milk
2 ice cubes
1–2 teaspoons honey (depending on sweetness of fruit)

Whirl all ingredients in a blender until smooth, pour into glass and enjoy. Serves one.

Variations:

For banana/wild strawberry smoothie, add a banana.

For a low-calorie version, use skim milk and fat-free yogurt.

For chocolate/wild strawberry smoothie, add a squirt of chocolate syrup.

Wild in the Kitchen

Lemon Tarts with Wild Strawberries

This recipe is for when you don't have quite enough wild strawberries to make a pie or jam, but you want to serve them to friends. Here is a way to show them off, but only a few of them are needed to make an impact!

Make 12–18 mini tarts using your favorite pastry recipe. Let cool.

Filling:

- 3 eggs, beaten
- 1 cup sugar
- juice and zest of 3–4 lemons (½ cup juice)
- ¼ cup butter
- ½ cup (or so) wild strawberries

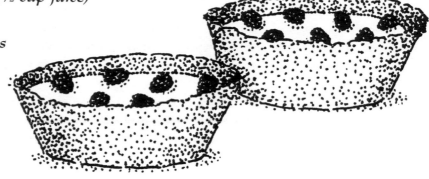

Combine all ingredients except the strawberries and bring them to a simmer and cook, stirring constantly until the mixture starts to thicken (about 10–12 minutes). Let cool. Put cooled lemon filling into tart shells.

Top each tart with 6 or 8 cleaned and hulled wild strawberries.

If there is any leftover lemon filling, seal it in a glass jar and put it in the refrigerator. Try it as a spread on your morning toast!

Variations:

Orange tarts: substitute ¼ cup lemon juice, ¼ cup freshly squeezed orange juice, and the zest of the lemon and orange for ½ cup lemon juice. (If you use only orange juice, the filling loses its tartness.)

Lime tarts: instead of ½ cup lemon juice, use ½ cup lime juice and the zest of the limes.

Wild Strawberry Fool

A "fool" is a traditional English dessert combining fruit purée and cream. In this case, the wild straw-berries are so petite, it is not really necessary to purée them.

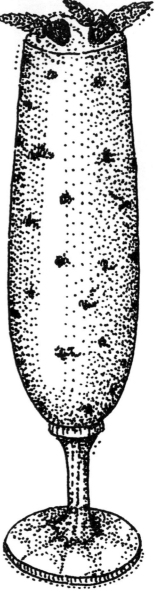

2 cups wild strawberries
½ cup sugar
juice of ½ lemon
2 cups heavy cream
1 teaspoon vanilla

Clean and remove stems from wild strawberries. Put them in a saucepan with the sugar and lemon juice and cook for 20 minutes over medium heat, stirring occasionally. Transfer mixture to a bowl and put in the refrigerator to cool. This can be done a day or two ahead of serving.

In a mixing bowl, whip cream and vanilla until soft peaks form. Fold strawberry mixture into the whipping cream. Do not overmix. Spoon into tall parfait glasses and garnish with 2 or 3 wild berries and mint leaves. Makes 4 servings.

 *Field Notes*

 Field Notes

Flowers

Clover

White, mauve, pink, or deep red, clover can be found everywhere—along country roads, in meadows and fields, even in back yards. The leaves and flowers of the clover are edible; in fact, it was used for medicinal purposes by native people and early settlers. A member of the pea family, this three-leafed plant (if you find one with four leaves, you might just have good luck!) is most tasty when quite young. Therefore, it's best to pass by those flowers that droop. Small blooms can be baked right into a white cake batter for a different sort of clover dessert. Or serve the blooms and leaves as a side dish. Just simmer in a bit of water for a couple of minutes, drain, and serve with salt, pepper, and butter.

Warning: When picking clover, be careful of bees!

Clover Blossom Vinegar

2–3 cups of purple clover, blossoms only
2 cups white vinegar
½ teaspoon salt
3 tablespoons sugar

Fill a jar with the clover blossoms. Bring the vinegar, salt, and sugar to a boil in a saucepan. Pour it over the blossoms, seal the jar, and let it stand overnight. Next morning, pour the liquid into a pot, reboil and pour it back into the jar, over the flowers. Repeat this for 5 consecutive days. You will notice that as the days progress, the flowers start to lose their color and the liquid takes on a lovely purple-pink shade. After you have finished this process, strain off the liquid through a cheesecloth and bottle it for use in salad dressings and vinaigrettes.

Pink Clover Vinaigrette

½ cup watermelon, cubed (no seeds or rind)
3 tablespoons Clover Blossom Vinegar
3 tablespoons olive oil
1 tablespoon honey
1 tablespoon fresh lemon juice, plus zest of 1 lemon
1 teaspoon fresh parsley, chopped
salt and pepper to taste

Put watermelon in food processor and purée. Add remaining ingredients and process. Makes about 1 cup of dressing. Can be bottled and stored in the refrigerator for up to a week.

Serving suggestion: fresh salad greens (a combination of any of the following: mesclun, spinach, beet tops, arugula, romaine or Boston lettuce) with mandarin orange slices (canned ones that have been drained very well work better than fresh mandarins), red onion rings, and sliced red peppers. Top with toasted almond slices. Pour some of the Pink Clover Vinaigrette on top and toss well.

Dandelion Flower Marmalade Jelly

This sharp-tasting recipe is strained so it becomes a jelly instead of a chunky marmalade. For more on dandelions, see page 84.

> *3 oranges*
> *2 lemons*
> *½ pound dandelion flowers (without stems or green ends)*
> *6 cups water*
> *sugar (quantity below)*

Cut oranges and lemons into wedges, without peeling them. Remove any seeds and put the fruit into a large pot. Wash and drain dandelion flowers and add them along with 6 cups of water. Simmer uncovered for one hour over low heat.

Pour liquid through a strainer into a large measuring pitcher and note quantity (discard fruit). Pour into large saucepan. Add sugar equivalent to the amount of liquid. Boil for one hour, stirring occasionally.

Pour into sterilized jars and seal. Process in a hot water bath (see pages 14–15 for instructions). Makes 2–3 half-pint (250 mL) jars.

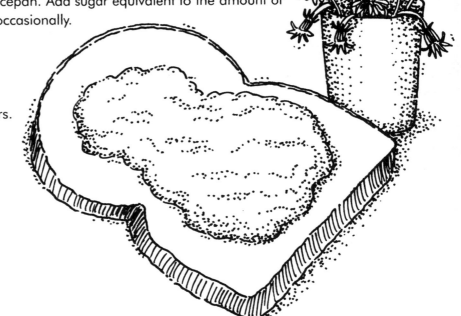

Wild in the Kitchen

Day Lilies

You may be growing them in your flower garden, but all over the countryside you'll find the beautiful orange day lily growing wild in ditches, along country roads, or at the perimeter of fields and meadows.

You can add the baby shoots to your salad or use the maturing flower buds. The flowers themselves can be made into fritters. If you want to thin out your wildflower bed, the cooked roots, once scraped, are edible and can be a good potato substitute.

Spicy Ginger Day Lily Buds

2 cups day lily buds
1 teaspoon coarse salt
4 2-inch pieces cinnamon stick
16 whole cloves
1 cup white vinegar
¼ cup water
2 tablespoons sugar
¼ cup chopped candied ginger
2 teaspoons ground ginger
¼ teaspoon hot red pepper flakes

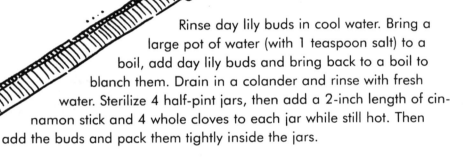

Rinse day lily buds in cool water. Bring a large pot of water (with 1 teaspoon salt) to a boil, add day lily buds and bring back to a boil to blanch them. Drain in a colander and rinse with fresh water. Sterilize 4 half-pint jars, then add a 2-inch length of cinnamon stick and 4 whole cloves to each jar while still hot. Then add the buds and pack them tightly inside the jars.

Meanwhile, in a saucepan, mix together the vinegar, water, sugar, candied ginger, ground ginger, and hot red pepper flakes. Bring to a boil and pour this mixture into each jar, leaving a half-inch head space. Run a plastic knife or non-metallic spatula around the inside of each jar to remove any air bubbles, and seal immediately with hot lids. Process in a hot water bath (see pages 14–15 for instructions).

Allow the flavors to meld for a month or two before opening. Makes 4 half-pint (250 ml) jars.

Steamed Day Lily Buds

In a medium-size saucepan fitted with a steamer, heat water to a boil. Add 1–2 cups of unopened day lily buds (whatever amount you have picked) to the steamer, cover and simmer for 3–4 minutes, or until tender. Drain and toss with butter, salt, and pepper. Serve piping hot. Try topping with grated Parmesan or even some hollandaise sauce.

Sautéed Day Lily Buds

Another way to serve the buds is to sauté them. Melt 1–2 tablespoons of butter in a large frying pan and fry the buds for 3–5 minutes or so, until the buds turn bright green and begin to open. Top with salt and pepper to taste.

Stuffed Day Lily Blossoms

Even though you start this recipe with fresh, open blooms, the petals close while they cook, to envelop the cheese stuffing within them. Serve these as an appetizer—they're a little hefty to serve as finger food (even though they come with their own handle!). Be sure to supply extra napkins as your guests will want to grab every bite.

12 open day lily blossoms
½ cup ricotta cheese
¼ cup mozzarella cheese, shredded
1 tablespoon Parmesan cheese
1 tablespoon fresh parsley, chopped
salt and pepper (to taste)
½–¾ cup flour
1 egg, beaten
1 tablespoon milk
2–4 tablespoons butter

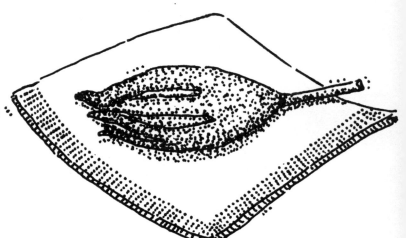

Check over the day lily flowers for bugs. Do not wash the flowers unless they appear dusty or dirty. Remove the stamens and pistil from the inside of the flower to make room for the filling. Snap them off carefully, as close as possible to the inside and discard. Set blossoms aside.

In a bowl, mix the ricotta, mozzarella, Parmesan, parsley, salt, and pepper until well combined. Take about 1 tablespoon of the mixture and stuff it into the cuplike cavity of the flower.

Put the flour onto a large plate. In a shallow bowl, mix the egg and milk together. Take the stuffed flower, holding it gently around its middle (to keep the filling contained), and roll it in the flour and then in the egg mixture. In a skillet, melt 2 tablespoons butter. Put the stuffed flower head into the pan and fry on medium-low heat until browned (about 2 minutes). Then flip it over and brown on the other side. Proceed with all the blossoms, adding butter to the frying pan as needed.

As the blossoms are cooking, place the completely browned ones onto a warm platter and keep in a low oven (200°F) until ready to serve. Makes 12 portions.

Elder Flower Bubbly

This is a flowery tasting, champagnelike beverage, made from the lovely white flowers of the blooming elder plant (see page 33 for information on the elder). If this drink fails to "bubble" when it is done, don't despair! Pour equal amounts of elder flower liquid with sparkling water or seltzer. Then it will be a sparkling beverage.

1 gallon water (16 cups)
3 cups sugar
2 tablespoons white vinegar
12 large elder flower heads
1 lemon

Place a large pot filled with water, sugar, and vinegar on the stove and put on medium heat. Stir until sugar is completely dissolved. Remove from heat and let cool a bit.

Strip the elder flowers off their large stems. Slice the lemon very thinly, leaving the skin on. Sterilize four quart (or liter) jars and distribute the flowers and the lemon slices evenly among them, placing them in the bottom of each jar. Ladle the cooled water mixture into each jar and seal tightly. Set aside for 10–14 days.

When ready to drink, strain the liquid through a sieve and you will have a delightful bubbly beverage.

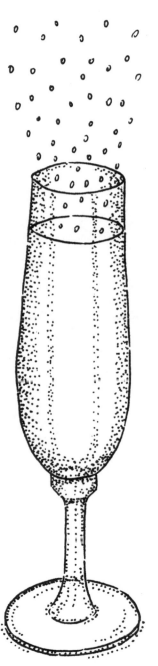

Sumac

Who would ever think that this crazy-looking bushlike tree would be the least bit edible? The staghorn sumac, which grows on hillsides all over the countryside, looks like Dr. Seuss drew it. You'll recognize it by the bright red cone (that looks like a fuzzy stag's horn) growing atop a bunch of fernlike leaves. The cone is made up of hairy berries growing tightly against each other, giving the cluster a velvety look. Once you've spotted the sumac, don't be impatient; wait for the fruit to turn deep crimson before harvesting (or else it is just too sour).

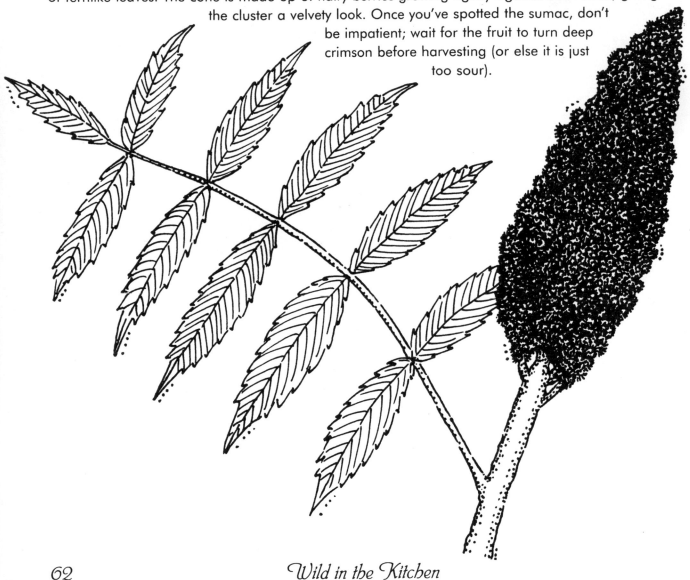

Wild in the Kitchen

Pink Sumac "Lemonade"

8 sumac horns
3 cups boiling water
sugar or honey (to taste)

Strip the berries from the main green stem into little treelike clusters. (The large green stem can make the mixture too bitter.) Put the berries into a large pot and cover with boiling water. Set aside to steep and cool. Strain carefully through a cheesecloth. Add sweetener to taste and serve over cracked ice with a few slices of lemon and sprigs of mint. Makes 2–3 glasses of lemonade.

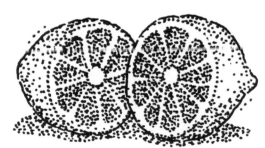

Sumac Spritzer

To make a bubbly refresher, put a few ice cubes into a tall glass. Fill the glass halfway with the prepared sumac lemonade (see above) and fill the rest of the glass with seltzer or sparkling water. Serve with sliced lemons or limes and a maraschino cherry.

Violets

"Roses are red, violets are blue . . ." But not always. Five-petaled violets vary in color from blue and purple to yellow and white. The lovely heart-shaped leaves and their edible flowers can be used fresh in a tossed salad or thrown into an omelet. The leaves are rich in vitamins A and C and are said to be a great laxative. So watch your intake! If you find yourself with extra blooms, pull out a jelly glass as a vase, fill it with water, and stuff it full of just-picked violets—a wonderful spring bouquet.

Wild in the Kitchen

Candied Violets

This is a great way to decorate a plain cake of any shape. Place the candied violets on your iced cake in an appealing pattern. These crystallized violets look great on white buttercream icing or dark chocolate frosting or even a glazed lemon loaf.

40 purple violet heads
⅓ cup superfine granulated sugar
   (see below)
1 egg white (lightly beaten)

Optional: purple or violet food coloring
   (paste or powder), to make the color
   last longer, as the natural color of
   the violets tends to fade

In a small bowl, mix the sugar with the food coloring (if you choose to use it). Try to get a uniform color, adding more coloring if necessary to deepen the shade.

With a small paintbrush, "paint" the beaten egg white onto the clean (and dry) violet petals, coating all sides. Hold the flower over the bowl of sugar and gently spoon the sugar over it, coating the entire violet. Shake off excess sugar and place on waxed paper–covered trays. Let dry thoroughly (about 24 hours). Store in airtight containers, in a cool, dark place.

Hint: If you are unable to find superfine granulated sugar, it is really easy to make your own. Put regular granulated sugar into a food processor with a metal blade and pulse until the sugar is superfine!

Field Notes

Fruits

Chokecherries

Chokecherries are common and widespread. They grow on small or tall bushes along hedgerows and fence lines and at the edges of forested areas. The plants are quite easy to recognize in springtime, when they are covered with flowers that grow in cylinder-shaped clusters that hang from the bushes like frilly decorations.

In late summer, these small red cherries turn to burgundy and nearly black . . . that is the best time to pick! When eaten raw, chokecherries are unpalatable and astringent and will make your mouth pucker. Perhaps this is why they are called "choke" cherries. But the fruit is wonderfully tasty when used in jellies and syrups; it produces a deep purplish red color when cooked.

When it is a good year for chokecherries, they are easy to pick and can be gathered very quickly. Fistfuls of cherries can fill buckets in no time flat. The only problem you might have is beating the birds to these tasty treats. When you are picking, bear in mind you are sharing nature's bounty with other creatures. Don't pick them all . . . leave a few for others in search of their dinner.

Never eat the pits or wilted leaves of the chokecherry. They contain hydrocyanic acid, so *do not eat them!* However, since cooking the fruit destroys the cyanide, pitting is unnecessary. If eating a raw chokecherry, be sure to spit out the pit!

Chokecherry and Pecan Conserve

Spreading this conserve on your morning toast is an elegant way to start your day.

5 cups chokecherries
½ cup water
3 medium apples, peeled and chopped
juice and zest of 1 orange
juice and zest of 1 lemon
2½ cups sugar
1 cup pecan halves

Wash and pick over chokecherries, removing any leaves. Do not remove tiny stems or pits. Put the chokecherries and water in a large pot and cook at medium-high, until the cherries are softened and split, about 10 minutes. Put through a food mill or heavy sieve, making sure to press the pulp through. This should yield about 1⅓ to 1½ cups juice and pulp.

Put juice and pulp into a clean pot. Then add the apples, the juice and zest of the orange and lemon, and the sugar. On high heat, bring to a full boil. Reduce heat to medium, stirring to make sure that the mixture doesn't stick. Skim foam off the top and discard. Keep boiling and stirring until the mixture starts to thicken, about 15–20 minutes. (It will be a soft set, like a thick pudding.) Add pecans and return to a boil for a minute. Bottle in hot, sterilized jars. Process in a hot water bath (see pages 14–15 for instructions). Makes 4 half-pint (250mL) jars.

Hot! Hot! Hot! Chokecherry Chutney

A great accompaniment to plain chicken, or spread it on your next grilled cheese sandwich for a real change.

6 cups chokecherries
2 apples, quartered
1 cup water
1½ cups brown sugar
1½ cups cider vinegar
1 tablespoon ground ginger
1 teaspoon salt
1 teaspoon cinnamon
½ teaspoon allspice
½ teaspoon ground cloves
½ teaspoon ground pepper
½ teaspoon cayenne pepper
2 tablespoons fresh ginger, minced
2 cloves garlic, minced
1 cup chopped onions
1 cup raisins

Wash the chokecherries well, discarding any leaves. Add them to a pot along with the apples. (Do not peel apples, but remove and discard blossom ends.) Add water and cook until the apples are soft, about 20 minutes. Put mixture into a food mill or strong sieve and push through juice and pulp. You should have a little over 2 cups of liquid and pulp.

Add liquid and pulp to a large pot along with all the other ingredients. Bring to a boil and then turn heat down to low. Slowly simmer mixture, uncovered, until it has thickened, about 1 to 1½ hours. Make sure to stir it often so it does not stick to the bottom of the pot. Pour into hot, sterilized jars and seal immediately. Process in a hot water bath (see pages 14–15 for instructions). Makes 3 half-pint (250 mL) jars.

Wild in the Kitchen

Chokecherry Marmalade

5 cups chokecherries

1 cup water

1 orange

2 lemons

2 tablespoons fresh ginger, grated

2 cups sugar

Wash the chokecherries well, but do not bother to remove the tiny stems or pits. Put them in a pot, along with the water, and cook for 10 minutes until the chokecherries have softened. Pour into a food mill or sieve and press the pulp and juice through. Yield should be about 2 cups.

Into a clean pot add the 2 cups of chokecherry juice and pulp. To that, add the orange and lemons, quartered and sliced very thin (peel and all, but discard the pits). Add the fresh ginger along with the sugar to the pot. Bring the mixture to a boil, then reduce heat and simmer gently for nearly an hour. Stir periodically to ensure that nothing sticks. When you can draw a spoon across the bottom of the pot and it leaves a clear channel (for a few seconds), your chokecherry marmalade is ready. Pour into sterilized jars immediately, and seal with hot lids. Process in a hot water bath (see pages 14–15 for instructions). Makes 3 half-pint (250 mL) jars.

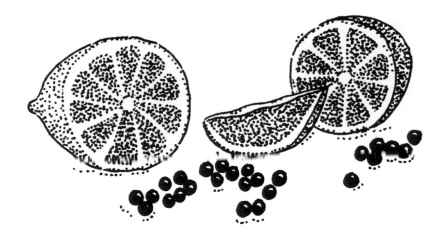

Crabapples and Wild Apples

Growing in rocky fields and abandoned lanes or along old fences, wild apples of various shapes and sizes can be found all over the countryside. In spring, their pink and white blooms cover the tree entirely. In the fall, their branches are heavy with fruit. Red, yellow, striped, green, speckled, spotted. That's just a short description of wild apples.

Wild crabapples are generally smaller than full-fledged wild apples but can often be found as big as 2 inches across. Crabapples are yellow, red, or both. They are too hard and tart to eat raw, but they are full of pectin and make a tasty jelly.

Wild apples are a painter's delight. And a gastronomic one, too. Each tree seems to bear fruit with a taste all its own. Try to overlook the fact that most are misshapen or scabby. These are not the apples you'll find at the grocery store! If you find several trees, take the time to taste each one. Some are mealy; others are sweet or tart. Take a selection of fruit home to make a different-tasting applesauce. Or chop some up into a cake batter. The possibilities with apples, especially wild ones, are limited only by your imagination.

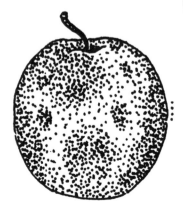

Spiced Crabapples

This savory recipe can be served as a side dish with poultry or chops.

> *4–5 pounds of crabapples*
> *2½ cups white vinegar*
> *2 cups water*
> *4 cups sugar*

In a cheesecloth bag:
> *1 tablespoon whole cloves*
> *3–4 cinnamon sticks*
> *1 3-inch piece of fresh, peeled ginger*

Wash and remove blossom ends of crabapples (leave the stems on). (You may insert a whole clove to fill this hole, but although it looks great, it is time consuming.) Prick each crabapple a few times, so that they don't burst while cooking.

Heat vinegar, water, and sugar to boiling in a large pot. Add the spices in the cheesecloth bag. Then add the crabapples and cook for 2–3 minutes. Remove the pot from the burner, cover, and set aside to cool overnight.

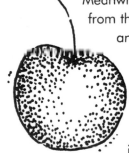

In the morning, sterilize jars in boiling water and pack apples into the hot jars (discard the spice bag). Meanwhile, heat the liquid from the pot to boiling and pour over fruit. Make sure there are no air bubbles and seal with hot lids. Process in a hot water bath for 30 minutes (see pages 14–15 for instructions). Makes 5–6 pint (500 mL) jars.

Wild Apple Butter

Spread this wonderful stuff onto hot toast for a mouthwatering breakfast.

> 4–5 pounds wild apples
> 2½ cups sweet apple cider
> 3–4 cups brown sugar (to taste)
> 2 teaspoons cinnamon
> ½ teaspoon ground cloves
> ½ teaspoon ground allspice
> juice and zest of 1 lemon
> juice and zest of 1 orange

Quarter the wild apples, but do not peel or core them. (Be sure to cut out all the wormy or bruised parts.) Put the apples into a large saucepan with the apple cider. Cook uncovered until soft, about 30 minutes. Strain pulp through a food mill or sieve, leaving behind the skin and seeds.

For each cup of purée, add about a half cup of brown sugar (taste it and see how sweet you like it). Add the spices and the juice and zest of the lemon and orange, and let it bubble over very low heat for 2–3 hours until thickened to a spreadable consistency. Stir it every half hour, to make sure it hasn't stuck to the bottom of the pot. Watch carefully, as this mixture can burn quite easily. Seal in hot, sterilized jars. Process in a hot water bath (see pages 14–15 for instructions). Makes 4–5 half-pint (250 mL) jars.

Wild Apple Pudding

The topping sauce envelops the wild apples in a caramel bath. Just delicious!

2 tablespoons butter
½ cup sugar
1 cup flour
1 teaspoon baking powder
1 teaspoon cinnamon
pinch of salt
2 cups wild apples, peeled and chopped
½ cup raisins or dried cherries
6 tablespoons milk

Topping:
¾ cup brown sugar
1 tablespoon butter
1½ cups boiling water
1 teaspoon vanilla

In a medium-sized mixing bowl, cream butter and sugar with a wooden spoon. In a separate bowl, mix together flour, baking powder, cinnamon, and salt. Then add chopped apples and raisins or cherries. Add the apple mixture to the creamed mixture alternately with the milk until everything is combined. Spread into a deep, 9-inch square (ungreased) dish and set aside.

For the topping: In a medium-sized bowl, add sugar, butter, and boiling water and stir until the sugar dissolves and the butter melts. Add the vanilla and pour over apple batter. Bake at 400°F for 30–35 minutes, until bubbly and brown on top. Let cool and top with a dollop of whipped cream. Serves 6–8.

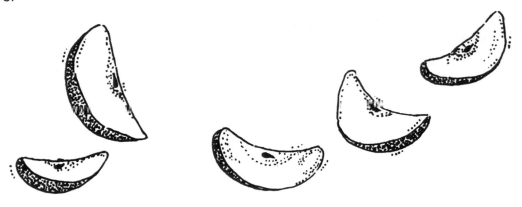

Wild Apple Chutney

1 tablespoon oil
1 tablespoon mustard seeds
1 onion, diced
1 red pepper, diced
1 tablespoon fresh ginger, grated
1 teaspoon salt
2 cups wild apples, peeled, cored, and chunked
½ teaspoon cinnamon
1 teaspoon ground ginger
1 teaspoon ground allspice
⅓ cup raisins
1 cup brown sugar
¾ cup red wine or cider vinegar
1 cup water

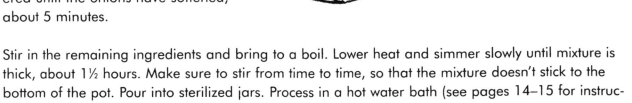

In a large saucepan, heat oil on high heat and add mustard seeds. Cover the pot and cook until the popping stops (this toasts the mustard seeds). Make sure not to burn them. Lower the heat and add onions, red pepper, fresh ginger, and salt. Over medium-low heat, cook uncovered until the onions have softened, about 5 minutes.

Stir in the remaining ingredients and bring to a boil. Lower heat and simmer slowly until mixture is thick, about 1½ hours. Make sure to stir from time to time, so that the mixture doesn't stick to the bottom of the pot. Pour into sterilized jars. Process in a hot water bath (see pages 14–15 for instructions). Makes 2 half-pint (250 mL) jars.

Wild Grapes

There are more than 50 native species of wild grapes growing in North America. They are smaller than their domestic cousins and a lot more tart! Wild grapes grow all over the countryside . . . on old fences and right up the trunks and branches of trees.

The leaves are large, coarsely toothed and somewhat heart shaped. They are edible and best when they are young, in spring or early summer.

The grapes themselves are very small and dark purple when ripe. Since they are fairly acidic, it is best to eat them cooked with sugar. Wild grapes are good in preserves, jelly, pies, and wine. They are sweetest after the first frost, but if you are making jelly, along with the purple fruit pick some green ones, as they contain pectin.

Avoid the poisonous Canada Moonseed, which looks similar to the wild grape. It grows on a vine but has no tendrils and its leaves are more rounded and not toothed like the wild grape. The Moonseed has a single, flattened seed inside its unpalatable fruit. The wild grape contains 2–4 roundish seeds.

Wild Grape Jelly

If you pick unripe (green) grapes along with the ripe (purple) ones, there will be enough pectin for this jelly to gel.

8–10 cups wild grapes
2 cups water
sugar (see below)
1 envelope pectin (optional)

Rinse wild grapes thoroughly in running water, discarding any moldy or spoiled fruit. Remove some of the larger stems, measure roughly, and put the grapes into a large pot. Mash the fruit with a potato masher and add water. Bring to a simmer for 15–20 minutes, until the fruit has softened. Strain the juice through a food mill or heavy sieve, leaving the stems, skins, and seeds behind. Discard these and set the juice aside in a pot, overnight.

Next morning, pour off the juice, leaving any crystals that might have formed at the bottom of the pot. Rinse the crystals out. Measure the juice back into the clean pot and add an equal quantity of sugar. Bring to a rolling boil until the gel point has been reached (about 15–20 minutes). Be sure to skim off any foam that may have formed on the surface. (If it doesn't gel at this point, you may need to add one envelope of pectin powder or liquid.)

Seal in sterilized jars. Process in a hot water bath (see pages 14–15 for instructions). Makes about 6–8 half-pint (250 mL) jars.

Wild in the Kitchen

Ground Cherries

The ground cherry is a member of the Nightshade family and perhaps less famous than its familiar cousins. The tomatillo used in Mexican cooking is one well-known relative, as is the decorative Chinese lantern plant with its bright orange lanterns. Another cousin is the Hawaiian poha. Its most famous kin is the tomato.

Ground cherries are also known as Cape gooseberries, husk tomatoes, or strawberry tomatoes. There are several wild species of the *Physalis* genus (the term *Physalis* is Greek for the "bladder" that surrounds the fruit), to which the ground cherry belongs, growing throughout most of the United States and Canada.

The plants sprawl across the ground, growing on top of grass or other weeds, to about 12 to 18 inches in length. They produce small bell-like flowers, which are pale yellow with a brownish interior. In midsummer, these flowers produce a five-sided green lantern, which contains a blueberry-sized fruit. Unripe, the berry is green, but when it ripens (in late summer or early fall) it turns orange-yellow. Many times, the paper husk, which turns brown when the fruit ripens, falls to the ground and gets lacy, freeing up the berry to be lost in the weeds. That is when the fruit is tastiest, so check the ground under the lantern. You'll usually find the fruit lying right underneath it.

Like the tomato, the ground cherry's leaves are poisonous. Some say the unripe fruit is as well, so be sure to pick the berries when they are yellow or orange and the lanterns are papery and antique looking. Avoid eating green berries.

Since the berry is filled with many tiny seeds, I save the overripe fruit (ones that have turned brown) to dry and plant in my own "wild" garden the next year.

Ground Cherry Jelly

This stuff is just wonderful. It has the consistency of honey and tastes a little like it, too.

2 cups ground cherries
Enough water to cover (about 2 cups)
1½–1¾ cups sugar
4–5 ground cherries, set aside for decoration

Remove paper lanterns and stems from the cherries and rinse clean. Add them to a small saucepan and add enough water to cover. Bring to a boil. Crush the cherries and let simmer until soft, about 15–20 minutes.

Pour the cooked cherries into a jelly bag and let drip. (I squeeze the bag to get all the juice possible, but this leads to a bit of a cloud in your jelly.) You'll end up with about 1¾ cups of juice. Put this into a clean pot, add about 1½–1¾ cups of sugar (depending on how sweet you like your jelly), and bring to a boil. Let this mixture simmer for about 15 minutes until gelling stage is reached. Pour into jelly glasses and seal.

If you'd like to add several ground cherries into the jelly, let it cool a bit until semiset. Then, in each jar insert 1 or 2 fresh ground cherries to float in the jelly. Push them into the jelly with a wooden skewer, making sure not to create any air pockets, and seal.

Process in a hot water bath (see pages 14–15 for instructions). Makes about 2 half-pint (250 mL) jars. For gifts, it might be a good idea to use the tiny quarter-pint (125 mL) jars so that more people can have a taste of this special jelly.

Field Notes

Field Notes

Wild
Greens

Dandelions

You've just mowed the lawn and are proud of the carpet of splendid greenery you've created. Then, in a matter of days, their yellow heads surface once more. Those darn dandelions!

But who says these bright yellow flowers have to go? One person's weed is another person's lunch. Dandelion leaves—picked young and tender—can be tossed into a salad or even stir-fried. Eating them is great way to get a healthy dose of vitamins A and C. Dandelion flower heads (minus the stems) can be made into a delicious marmalade jelly (see page 56 for the recipe).

Naturally, avoid dandelions growing on lawns that have been sprayed with chemicals.

Wild in the Kitchen

Braised Dandelion Greens with Blue Cheese and Almonds

1 tablespoon oil

1 onion, chopped

8–10 cups young dandelion greens, chopped

3 tablespoons raspberry vinegar (recipe on page 45)

2 tablespoons water

3 teaspoons sugar

salt and pepper (to taste)

¼ cup sliced almonds, toasted lightly until golden brown

¼ cup blue cheese, crumbled

In a large saucepan, add oil and onions and cook on medium-low heat, about 5 minutes, until soft and transparent (do not brown). Add the chopped dandelion greens and stir until the greens are wilted, about 5 minutes. Add raspberry vinegar, water, and sugar to the pan, and cook until the greens are tender (about 5 minutes). Season with salt and pepper.

Put dandelion greens into a serving dish and top with toasted sliced almonds and crumbled blue cheese. Makes 2–4 servings.

Wilted Dandelion Salad

By tossing hot dressing through the dandelion greens, they wilt a bit and make for a very unusual warm salad.

6 cups dandelion greens
6 slices bacon
2 tablespoons bacon fat (or olive oil)
1 clove of garlic, minced
5 tablespoons red wine vinegar
1 teaspoon sugar
salt and pepper (to taste)
1 hard-boiled egg

dandelion greens

garlic

Wash and dry the dandelion greens very well. Chop them into 2-inch pieces, put them in a large bowl, and set aside.

Fry 6 slices of bacon until very crisp. Put the bacon on a paper towel to drain. Pour off all the fat from the frying pan and measure 2 tablespoons of it back into the pan. (You can substitute olive oil for the bacon fat.) Put over low heat and add the minced garlic. While frying the garlic, scrape the pan to get all the tasty brown bits off the bottom. Cook the garlic until softened but not burned (about 3–5 minutes). Remove the pan from the stove and add the wine vinegar. (Stand back because it might splash!) Return the pan to the burner and add the sugar, salt, and pepper. Heat through and pour on top of the dandelion greens. Toss well.

hard boiled egg

crisp bacon

Crumble up the crisp bacon and add it to the salad. Remove the yolk from the hard-boiled egg (discard the white part). With a wooden spoon, push the yolk through a fine sieve to crumble it. Toss it through the salad. Add more salt and pepper to taste and serve the wilted salad while it is still warm. Makes enough for 6–8 servings.

Fiddleheads

Fiddleheads grow in moist areas along the edge of rivers and swamps in early spring. Actually, fiddleheads are the very beginning of the growth of a fern; in about two weeks they will unfurl to become the leaves of an inedible plant. It is important to identify the fiddlehead you pick as being the onset of the Ostrich fern. When fully grown, these ferns grow in vaselike clumps, about 2 to 6 feet tall. You might have to check these out the summer before you pick them so you know what you are picking the following spring. At any rate, always check your field guide carefully as all ferns emerge in the fiddlehead formation. Ferns other than Ostrich could be toxic.

To clean your fiddleheads, place them in a brown paper bag and shake well. Or brush off their papery sheaths with a mushroom brush. Rinse well in cool water.

And be sure to wear your rubber boots when collecting. You might even tuck an extra pair of socks in your pocket, on your way to pick. Every time I've picked fiddleheads, water inevitably goes over the top of one of my boots.

Fiddlehead Pickles

4 pounds fiddleheads
4 cups water
½ cup white vinegar
¼ cup coarse salt
1 teaspoon sugar

In each jar put the following:
1 garlic clove
1 bay leaf
3 whole peppercorns
½ teaspoon pickling spice

Remove brown husks from fiddleheads and wash and trim ends to 1 inch or so from rolled-up coil. Blanch the fiddleheads in boiling water for 5–7 minutes, or until tender but not mushy. Then drain them well.

Place 4 cups of water in a saucepan; add vinegar, salt, and sugar. Bring to a boil.

Sterilize 8 half-pint jars. Put spices in each jar, then pack the fiddleheads tightly into the jars. Pour the hot vinegar mixture into each jar, leaving a half-inch head space. Make sure to remove any air bubbles that might be trapped by running the handle of a wooden spoon around the inside of the jar. Place hot lids on jars and tighten. Process in a hot water bath (see pages 14–15 for instructions). Makes 8 half-pint (250 mL) jars. Wait a few weeks before eating, to let the flavors mellow.

Sautéed Fiddleheads

25–30 fiddleheads
3 tablespoons butter
salt and freshly ground pepper
fresh lemon juice

Clean fiddleheads by removing the brown paperlike sheath from them. Wash them carefully in several baths of cold water and trim ends if necessary. Put fiddleheads in a pot fitted with a steamer and steam them covered, for 5 minutes. Remove them from the pot and drain in a colander.

Melt butter in a frying pan, add fiddleheads, and sauté for 1–2 minutes over medium heat, turning them in the pan. Season with salt, pepper, and a squirt of lemon juice, and serve piping hot.

You may also let them cool and serve them at room temperature or chilled with a nice vinaigrette.

Cream of Fiddlehead Soup

2 tablespoons butter
1 onion, chopped
1 clove garlic
1½ pounds fiddleheads, coarsely chopped
4½ cups chicken broth
1 teaspoon salt
¼ teaspoon pepper
½ cup half-and-half or milk
fresh parsley or chives (optional)

In a large pot, melt butter. Add onions and garlic and cook until softened (do not brown), about 5 minutes. Add fiddleheads and sauté for 5 minutes. Add chicken broth, salt, and pepper and simmer for 5–10 minutes, until the fiddleheads are bright green and cooked but not mushy.

Purée half the soup in a blender or food processor until smooth and return to pot. Add the half-and-half or milk and heat through, about 5 minutes.

Ladle into bowls and snip fresh parsley or chives on top. Makes about 6 servings.

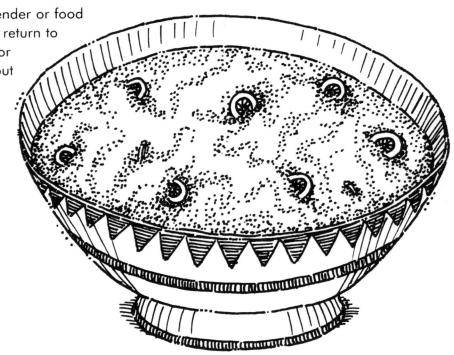

Wild in the Kitchen

Meat-Stuffed Wild Grape Leaves

Tender, young grape leaves can be steamed for 10 minutes; topped with butter, salt, and pepper; and served as a side dish (like spinach). But they are best when stuffed with various fillings, to make wonderful appetizers. For more information on wild grapes, see page 77.

40–50 young grape leaves (pick extra for lining the pan and in case of tearing)
1 teaspoon olive oil (plus extra)
1 onion, finely chopped
1 pound ground veal (ground beef or pork may be
*   substituted, but drain the fat)*
¼ cup cooked rice
salt and pepper (to taste)
2 tablespoons fresh parsley, chopped
3 tablespoons fresh mint, chopped
juice and zest of 2 lemons

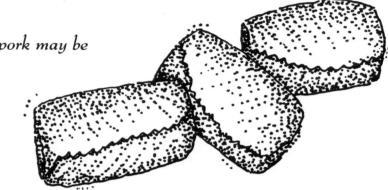

Take fresh grape leaves, remove stems, and blanch in salted, boiling water for 3 minutes. Then rinse them in cold water, drain well, and set aside.

In a frying pan, add olive oil and chopped onions. Sauté a few minutes, until the onions have softened. Add the ground meat and brown well. Remove the pan from the heat, drain any fat, add cooked rice, salt, and pepper. Mix well.

Place a softened grape leaf, vein side up with the stem end toward you on a work surface. Put about 1 tablespoon of the meat mixture at the point where the veins branch out. Starting with the stem end, roll up the leaf, then tuck in the sides and continue rolling, making a tight packet. Rub the entire surface of a deep pot with olive oil. Place a few grape leaves on the bottom of the pot to cover it. Place rolled packets tightly together along the bottom of the pot. Cover that layer with flat leaves, some chopped parsley, mint, and lemon rind. Add another layer of stuffed, rolled leaves, and cover in the same way. Repeat this until all the stuffed leaves are in the pot. Add ¼ cup water to pot. Cover the top with a lid or heavy ovenproof plate. Simmer over low heat, tightly covered, for 1 hour. (Make sure the heat is low as the contents might scorch if the heat is too high.) Remove pot from heat and uncover.

Preheat oven to 350°F. Arrange stuffed leaves in a well-oiled baking dish. Sprinkle with lemon juice and some of the liquid from the pot. Bake, uncovered, for 30 minutes or until almost all the liquid is gone. Can be served warm or cold. Makes 30–35 appetizers.

Orange-and-Currant-Stuffed Wild Grape Leaves

60 grape leaves
4–6 tablespoons olive oil
1 onion, chopped
¾ cup long grain and wild rice mix, uncooked
½ teaspoon ground allspice
½ teaspoon cinnamon
¼ cup currants
1¾ cups water
1¼ cup pine nuts, toasted
zest and juice of 2 lemons and 1 orange

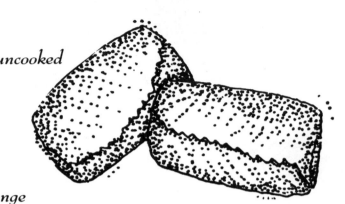

Take fresh grape leaves, remove stems, and blanch in boiling, salted water for 3 minutes. Then rinse with cold water and set aside to drain. Meanwhile, heat 2 tablespoons of olive oil in a medium-sized saucepan over medium heat. Sauté chopped onions until tender, about 5 minutes. Add rice (do not use seasoning packet), allspice, cinnamon, and currants, and cook for one minute longer. Add water and bring to a boil. Reduce heat to low, cover and let simmer until the rice is cooked and the water is absorbed (about 20–25 minutes). Let cool.

Place pine nuts on a cookie sheet and toast in a 300°F oven for 3–5 minutes, until the nuts are golden brown, stirring occasionally. Let them cool. Chop the nuts and add to the rice mixture. Add finely diced zest of the lemons and orange (save juice for later) and stir.

Cover the bottom of a heavy, large frying pan with 8–10 grape leaves, running them up the sides of the pan. (This will prevent the stuffed leaves from sticking to the frying pan.)

Place one softened grape leaf, vein side up, stem side toward you on your work surface. Place approximately a teaspoonful of rice mixture in middle of leaf and roll away from you halfway, tuck in sides, and continue rolling until you have a neat, tight package. Place stuffed leaves, seam side down, closely together in the leaf-lined frying pan. Drizzle 2 tablespoons of olive oil on top of the stuffed grape leaves. Add juice of lemons and orange (about ¾ cup of liquid) and bring to a boil. Reduce heat to low, cover and simmer for 40 minutes or until all the liquid is absorbed. (Make sure to watch to avoid scorching.) Let cool. Makes 45–50 appetizers.

Labrador Tea

This low shrub grows to about 3 feet high and can be found in bogs and peaty wetlands of the northeastern United States and Canada. Its leathery-looking leaves are 1 to 2 inches long and have rolled edges. The backs of the leaves are white or rusty colored and have a woolly feel to them.

Since this is an evergreen plant, the leaves can be harvested in all four seasons to make an aromatic tea. It can be served hot or iced. (The flowers, however, are not edible.)

A great alternative to imported black tea, Labrador tea has no caffeine and is said to be a mildly narcotic tonic, used by pioneers and natives for treating coughs and other irritations, and in childbirth.

A Nice Cup of Labrador Tea

For storage purposes, Labrador tea leaves can be dried. Lay the leaves on a cookie sheet and place in a slow oven until crispy. Put the cooled leaves into a glass jar and store in a cool, dark cupboard.

Chop fresh Labrador tea leaves into small pieces (if using dried leaves, crumble them). Measure about one heaping teaspoon of leaves for each cup of water (or for each person served). Pour boiling water over tea leaves and let the mixture infuse for 5–10 minutes. (Don't boil the leaves in the water as it may release a harmful alkaloid.) The tea will be a pale shade of yellow-green when ready. Serve with honey, a lemon slice, or a sprig of mint.

LABRADOR TEA

Wild in the Kitchen

Lamb's Quarters

These weeds seem to grow everywhere . . . in vacant lots, roadsides, wastelands, and especially in your garden. But next time, don't throw them into your compost pile.

Lamb's quarters taste wonderful—sort of like wild spinach (which is one of its nicknames, along with "goosefoot" and "pigweed"). The diamond-shaped leaves are said to look like the leg of a lamb, hence its name. Others say it looks like a goose's foot. Why pigweed? I suppose pigs like the taste of this plant as much as humans do.

The plants can grow as high as 6 or 8 feet tall and are plentiful all over the United States and Canada. The seeds are abundant (as many as 75,000 seeds have been found on a single plant!) and appear in late summer or early fall. They can be used as a cereal food in bread or pancakes. They also can be dried in a slow oven until crisp and then pounded into flour.

But best of all is the taste of the greens. The leaf itself is unusual, as it seems to have a coating on it impossible to make wet (water beads up and rolls right off it). The foliage of the lamb's quarters is delicious all summer long. Just pick the small leaves that keep appearing on taller plants or find a plant under one foot tall and pick those leaves.

Unlike many other wild greens, lamb's quarters do not have an inherently bitter taste, nor are they tough or stringy. They don't need a lot of preparation time to make them ready to eat. Add lamb's quarters shredded raw to salads. Or steam them like spinach, which can be eaten immediately or frozen for winter use.

Lamb's Quarters and Cheese Pie

An interesting spin on the classic Greek spanakopita, which generally uses spinach as its leafy green. Go wild and try this instead!

1 pound lamb's quarters
1 tablespoon butter
2 medium onions, chopped
1 cup feta cheese, crumbled
½ pound (1 cup) dry cottage (or pot) cheese
3 eggs
¼ teaspoon nutmeg
1 teaspoon dried dill weed
salt and pepper to taste
½ cup butter, melted
1-pound package of phyllo dough, defrosted

Separate the leaves from the stems of the lamb's quarters; discard stems and wash the leaves well. Steam lamb's quarters for 5 minutes on stovetop or 2–3 minutes in the microwave, without adding any extra water (there is enough water from washing them). Let cool and remove any excess water by squeezing out the lamb's quarters. Chop coarsely and set aside.

Put 1 tablespoon of butter and the onions in a frying pan, cover, and let the onions "sweat" (get soft and not brown) over low heat for 10 minutes or so. Set aside to cool.

With an electric mixer, beat together the 2 cheeses, eggs, nutmeg, dill, salt, and pepper until incorporated. (Go easy on the salt as the feta cheese is quite salty.) Add softened onions, then the lamb's quarters. Beat all together.

Brush melted butter in the bottom and sides of a 9 × 13-inch pan. Put the first phyllo sheet at the bottom and nudge it in to fit (with the edges of the phyllo left hanging outside the pan). Brush with melted butter. Then keep layering the phyllo dough, brushing each sheet with butter, one at a time, until you have 8 sheets. Add half the filling and spread it evenly. Then continue with the phyllo dough and butter with 8 more sheets. Add the rest of the filling and top it off with more layers of phyllo and butter (roughly 6–8 sheets left in the package). Top with butter. Turn the edges up, making a border, and press it in place.

Bake in a 375°F oven, uncovered, for 45 minutes, until golden brown. Makes 6–8 servings.

Wild in the Kitchen

Lamb's Quarters and Sun-Dried Tomato Pasta

spaghetti or spaghettini, enough for 2 servings
1 tablespoon butter
1 tablespoon olive oil
1 onion, chopped
½ pound lamb's quarters
¼ cup sun-dried tomatoes
¼ cup Asiago (or very sharp cheddar) cheese, grated
salt and pepper
3 tablespoons Parmesan or Romano cheese
¼ cup pine nuts, toasted

Bring a large pot of water to a boil, add pasta, and cook following package instructions.

In a large frying pan, melt butter and add olive oil. Add chopped onion and sauté for 5 minutes or until soft. Add cleaned lamb's quarters and fry for another 5 minutes.

Meanwhile, rehydrate sun-dried tomatoes in boiling water for 5 minutes. (If they are preserved in oil, drain them.) Coarsely chop tomatoes and add to lamb's quarters.

Drain pasta in a colander and put in a large serving bowl. Add lamb's quarters mixture and toss it through the pasta. Add the grated Asiago cheese (use a sharp, aged cheddar if you can't find Asiago), salt, and pepper to taste. Top with Parmesan and toasted pine nuts. Serves 2.

White Bean and Lamb's Quarters Soup

2 tablespoons oil
2 cloves garlic
1 teaspoon chopped fresh rosemary
5–6 cups lamb's quarters
2 cans (15.5 oz. or 540 mL) white kidney (or cannellini) beans
2 cans (10 oz. or 284 mL) chicken broth
2 cups water
6 slices baguette or french bread, ½-inch thick
1 teaspoon fresh chives, chopped (optional)

Heat the oil with one clove of minced garlic (reserve the other clove for later) in a large pot. Add the chopped rosemary and fry on low for 2 minutes, until the garlic has softened (do not brown). Add the washed lamb's quarters, cover, and cook for 5 minutes on low, until the lamb's quarters have wilted. Then add one can of drained white beans.

Drain the second can of beans and mash or purée them in a food processor. Add them to the pot along with the chicken broth and water. Simmer, uncovered, for 10–15 minutes.

Meanwhile, toast the slices of bread and rub one side of each with the remaining clove of garlic. Place one slice of toast in the bottom of each soup bowl. Pour hot soup on top of toast (sprinkle each bowl with chopped chives, if you wish). Serve immediately. Makes 6 servings.

WHITE KIDNEY BEA

Wild in the Kitchen

Milkweed

Milkweed is fairly common and grows on roadsides and in fields. Many farmers consider it a noxious weed and have tried to eradicate it. Unfortunately, it is the major food source for the monarch butterfly.

For humans, nearly every part of the milkweed plant is edible—and tasty, too. But it bleeds a bitter, milky-white juice (hence the name "milkweed"). Luckily this bitterness can be blanched away (see below), and once this is done, the possibilities are endless.

In early spring, the young shoots are edible and can be used like asparagus. Later on in the season, you can eat the unopened flower buds, which are similar to broccoli. Summer comes and the pink flowers appear. These can be dipped in batter and fried as fritters. In midsummer, the unripe seed pods can be eaten as a vegetable or stuffed as hors d'oeuvres.

To blanch milkweed: Prepare a large pot of boiling water. Keep it boiling throughout this procedure. Place the milkweed in a smaller pot; pour boiling water from the larger pot over it. Boil the smaller pot for one minute, then drain it. Fill the small pot again with boiling water from the larger pot and boil once more for a minute. Repeat this step 3 or 4 times. Do not use fresh cold water and bring to a boil in the smaller pot. If you do, bitterness will set into the milkweed.

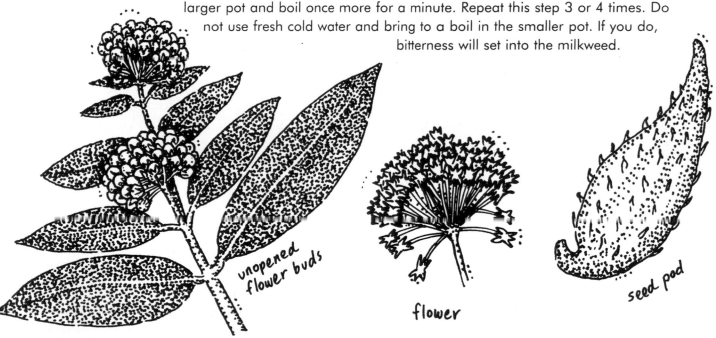

unopened flower buds

flower

seed pod

Milkweed "Broccoli" Salad

Salad:

    30 or more clusters of milkweed flower buds

    1 can of baby corn, drained and cut into bite-size pieces

       (frozen or canned corn kernels can be substituted)

    ½ red pepper, cubed

    1 slice of sweet onion, chopped

Vinaigrette:

    ½ cup good olive oil

    ½ teaspoon fresh parsley, chopped

    ¼ cup lemon juice

    ½ teaspoon fresh dill, chopped

    1 teaspoon Dijon mustard

    ¼ teaspoon salt

    ½ teaspoon sugar

    a few grinds of fresh pepper

    1 garlic clove, crushed

Blanch the cleaned flower buds. After blanching 3 or 4 times, bring the buds to a boil again and test after 3–5 minutes. (You want the bitter taste eliminated, but you don't want the buds to turn to mush.) When they are tender, pour cold water over them to stop further cooking. Put them in a salad spinner to remove most of the water, or in one or two tea towels and shake dry (don't squish them). Put the clusters into a bowl.

Add the baby corn, the cubed red pepper, and the sweet onion. Toss lightly to mix, pour vinaigrette dressing on top, and incorporate it into the salad. Serve cold or at room temperature. Serves 4 as a side salad.

To Make Vinaigrette: Put all the ingredients in a tightly covered jar and shake well to blend. Test before you pour it on the salad as it might need adjusting, according to your personal taste.

Chinese-Style Stir-Fried Milkweed

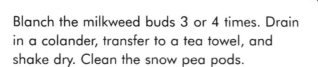

½–¾ *pound milkweed buds*
¼ *pound snow pea pods*
1 *teaspoon sesame oil*
1 *tablespoon soy sauce*
½ *teaspoon honey*
1 *tablespoon white vinegar*
1 *teaspoon hoisin sauce*
1 *tablespoon vegetable oil,*
   for frying
2 *teaspoons sesame seeds*

Blanch the milkweed buds 3 or 4 times. Drain in a colander, transfer to a tea towel, and shake dry. Clean the snow pea pods.

In a small dish mix sesame oil, soy sauce, honey, vinegar, and hoisin sauce together and stir well. Heat 1 tablespoon vegetable oil in frying pan or wok until hot. Add the milkweed buds and stir fry for 2–3 minutes. Add pea pods and continue frying for another minute. Pour sauce on top and stir-fry quickly until all the sauce has combined with the green vegetables. Put into a serving bowl and sprinkle sesame seeds on top. Serves 4–6 as a side dish.

Variations:
Any of the following may be added and stir-fried: strips of red pepper, cubed tofu, thinly sliced scallions, water chestnuts, bamboo shoots, and/or mung bean sprouts.

Cheesy Milkweed Pod Hors d'Oeuvres

24 (plus a few extra) milkweed pods (2 inches or less in length)
½ cup mushrooms, chopped
2 scallions, chopped
4 tablespoons cornflake crumbs (or bread crumbs)
2 tablespoons sour cream or plain yogurt
salt and pepper (to taste)
3–4 tablespoons freshly grated Parmesan cheese

Blanch the milkweed pods in 3 or 4 changes of boiling water. Then boil the pods for 3–5 minutes until tender and bright green. Drain and rinse with cold water (to stop them from cooking any more), and dry on a tea towel.

Slit the milkweed pods down one side, remove the contents into a bowl and chop it finely. (Set the pods aside.) To the bowl add the rest of the ingredients except the Parmesan cheese. Stir together. Then stuff the empty pods with this filling. Lay them on a foil-covered baking sheet and top each pod with a sprinkle of Parmesan. Bake in a 400°F oven for 8–10 minutes (the Parmesan should be lightly browned and the insides of the pods should be warm). Makes 24 hors d'oeuvres.

Wild in the Kitchen

Mint

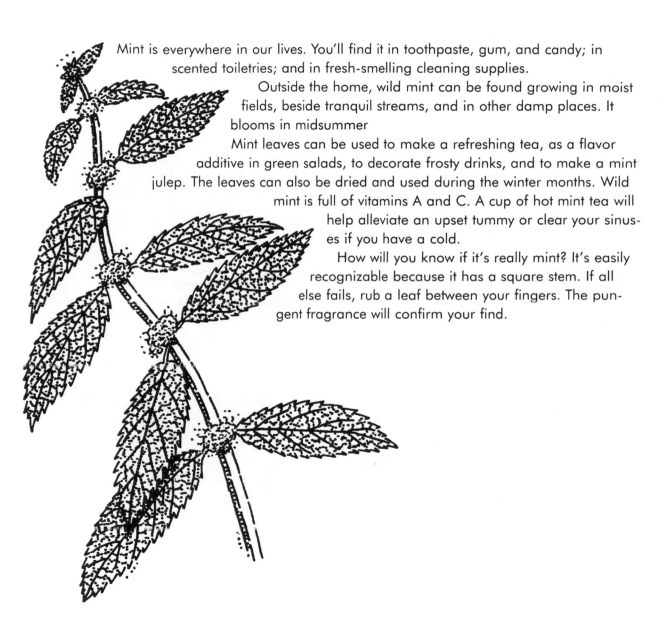

Mint is everywhere in our lives. You'll find it in toothpaste, gum, and candy; in scented toiletries; and in fresh-smelling cleaning supplies.

Outside the home, wild mint can be found growing in moist fields, beside tranquil streams, and in other damp places. It blooms in midsummer

Mint leaves can be used to make a refreshing tea, as a flavor additive in green salads, to decorate frosty drinks, and to make a mint julep. The leaves can also be dried and used during the winter months. Wild mint is full of vitamins A and C. A cup of hot mint tea will help alleviate an upset tummy or clear your sinuses if you have a cold.

How will you know if it's really mint? It's easily recognizable because it has a square stem. If all else fails, rub a leaf between your fingers. The pungent fragrance will confirm your find.

Sunny Mint Iced Tea

Instead of the standard boiling water, this iced tea recipe uses fresh cold water and the sun to make tea. It doesn't go cloudy when refrigerated, like boiled tea tends to do, and the taste is fresh and clean. Just fill a quart jar with the following:

10 stalks of wild mint, 8 to 10 inches in length
4 tea bags (orange pekoe is best)
1 quart of water

Put the jar in a sunny location in the morning and let the tea steep in the bright sunshine, for 4–6 hours. It will become a lovely, rich color. Remove the tea bags and the mint and put the jar in the refrigerator. Once chilled, serve over ice, garnished with wild mint leaves and a slice of lemon. Or serve with wild mint ice cubes (recipe follows).

Wild Mint Ice Cubes

Collect and clean 20 wild mint leaves, separating them from their stalks. Put a leaf or two into each section of an ice cube tray. Cover with water and put in freezer. After 2 or 3 hours, check the leaves and poke them deeper into the partially frozen water (the leaves tend to float up to the top of the tray). When completely frozen, put some of the cubes into a glass and pour iced tea over them. These flavorful cubes will give a lovely taste to any iced tea or cold beverage.

Wild in the Kitchen

Wild Mint Sauce

1 cup packed wild mint leaves
¼ cup cider vinegar
4 teaspoons sugar
2 tablespoons boiling water

Rinse mint thoroughly to remove any sand. Remove leaves from tough stems and chop mint finely to make one cup. In a medium-size bowl, mix chopped mint with remaining ingredients and let stand for one hour or more. Serve in a gravy boat with a ladle, in order to scoop up some of the mint leaves with the sauce.

Wild Mint Jelly

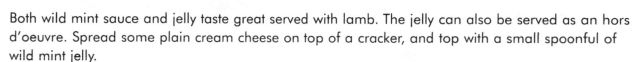

Both wild mint sauce and jelly taste great served with lamb. The jelly can also be served as an hors d'oeuvre. Spread some plain cream cheese on top of a cracker, and top with a small spoonful of wild mint jelly.

2 cups tightly packed mint leaves, plus some stems
2 cups water
¼ cup lime juice
3½ cups sugar
1 envelope liquid or powdered pectin

Coarsely chop the mint leaves and stems and place then in a medium saucepan. Add the water and bring to a boil. Stir occasionally and let simmer for 5 minutes. Remove from heat and set aside until cool (about 2 hours or so). Then strain through a sieve or cheesecloth, pressing the leaves to extract as much flavor as possible.

Measure the mint liquid and add 1¾ cups of it into a pot. Then add the lime juice and sugar. Bring to a boil and stir to make sure all the sugar has dissolved. Add the pectin, return to a boil, and let it boil for one minute. Then remove it from the heat. Skim off any foam that has formed on the top of the jelly. Pour it into hot, sterilized jars and seal immediately. Process in a hot water bath (see pages 14–15 for instructions). Makes 3 half-pint (250 mL) jars.

Tabouli Salad

This salad tastes great stuffed into fresh pita bread.

1 cup bulgur wheat
2 cups boiling water
2 ripe tomatoes
6 scallions (white and green parts), sliced
¼ cup wild mint leaves
2 cups parsley
½ cup lemon juice
¼ cup olive oil
½ teaspoon salt
pepper to taste

parsley

scallions

wild mint

Put uncooked bulgur wheat into a heat-proof bowl and pour boiling water into it. Stir and set aside for about an hour. Then drain well.

Finely dice the tomatoes and put in a large bowl. Add the scallions. Strip the leaves off the stems of the wild mint (discard stems) and chop leaves finely. Chop the parsley, too (trying to omit the large stems), and add both to the bowl. Add the lemon juice, oil, salt, and pepper and stir together. Then add cooked bulgur and mix thoroughly. Chill for 2 hours. Serves 6–8 people.

tomatoes

Wild in the Kitchen

Mustard

It is hard to miss the yellow fields blanketing the countryside in late spring or early summer. The culprit: mustard. It's one of the most familiar weeds worldwide and is a relative of the cabbage, radish, and turnip (which is why it has a peppery taste).

Early in spring, the first basal leaves of the mustard plant are tender and can be served after steaming for about 15–20 minutes. (They reduce in bulk quite a bit, so pick more than you think you can eat.) Drain well and add salt, pepper, and butter and serve as a side dish, or add it to vegetable soup.

Clusters of the unopened flower buds can also be steamed briefly (for 3–5 minutes) and served as a vegetable, as you would broccoli. (Make sure not to include any upper-stem leaves while you are picking, as they are extremely bitter.) Seed pods can be pickled (recipe follows) and the seeds themselves are conventionally added to most pickle recipes. If you grind the seeds, you get mustard powder, the key ingredient in table mustard.

The entire mustard plant is good for you. It is rich in vitamins A, B, and C, and the flower buds are rich in protein. The leaves are rich in calcium, phosphorus, and potassium.

Mustard-Seed-Pod Pickles

Strip the seed pods off the mustard plants while the bright yellow flowers are still in bloom at the top or the pods will be too tough to eat. A grocery-sized plastic bag full of stalks and flowers will yield about half a pound of seed pods . . . a bit of an arduous task to pick off the tiny pods, but these little guys are nice and peppery. Try them as a relish or pickle with poultry or fish.

½ pound mustard seed pods
2 cups white vinegar
½ cup water
6 teaspoons honey
1 teaspoon coarse salt
4 teaspoons pickling spice
5 garlic cloves, halved

In a colander, rinse the seed pods with cool water, making sure to remove any sand. Bring a pot of lightly salted water to a boil, add the seed pods, and return to a boil. Let cook a minute or so. Drain and set aside.

Mix together the vinegar, water, honey, salt, and pickling spice in a pot and bring to a boil. In hot sterilized jars, put 2 halves of garlic cloves; stuff the jars tightly with bright green seed pods. Then pour in the hot vinegar mixture, leaving a half-inch head space. Run a plastic knife or nonmetallic spatula around the jars to remove any air bubbles and seal tightly with sterilized covers. Process in a hot water bath (see pages 14–15 for instructions).

Let flavors mellow for a month or more before opening. Makes 5 half-pint (250 mL) jars.

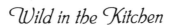
Wild in the Kitchen

Plantain and Purslane

Both of these leafy plants are common lawn and garden weeds.

Plantain has oval leaves that grow 6 to 8 inches long and about half as wide. The leaves taste best in the spring (at about 2 inches long), when young and tender. Otherwise their veins get too tough and stringy. The small leaves can be added to salads, cooked as greens, or put into soups. The flowering spikes, full of tiny seeds, can be dried and saved for bird food in winter.

Purslane is native to Persia or India and is prevalent in nearly every part of Canada and the United States. This succulent plant can be enjoyed from spring through fall. It is ground hugging, rarely growing higher than 2 inches, but can spread horizontally a foot or more. And purslane is good for you, too. It's rich in iron and contains vitamins A and C, calcium, and phosphorus.

Purslane leaves can be eaten raw in a salad, cooked as a green vegetable, pickled, or frozen. They have a quality that is rather sticky and moist. Throw a few leaves into your salad and see how your guests react. Most people like the mucilaginous quality, as it is refreshing and very different. When purslane leaves are cooked, they are a little like okra (they get mushy) and tend to fatten up a stock or stew, giving it a thicker consistency. Try pickling the stems by using them instead of cucumbers in your favorite dill pickle recipe.

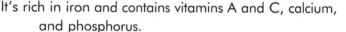

plantain

purslane

Wild and Crazy Soup

This soup never comes out the same way twice. That's because it depends on what you find in your refrigerator and what's available from the wild.

In a large pot, over medium heat, add:

> *2 teaspoons oil*

Look in the refrigerator and add to the pot any or all of the following:

> *1 onion, chopped*
> *celery leaves, chopped*
> *several carrots, shredded or chopped*
> *3 or 4 mushrooms, chopped*

Let these ingredients sweat in the oil and release their flavors. This should take about 10 minutes.

Add 6–8 cups of water or chicken stock to the pot. Then, go outside and see what you can find. Add some or most of the following:

> *¼ cup purslane leaves*
> *5 or 6 dried day lily heads*
> *a handful of shredded lamb's quarters*
> *a few small plantain leaves*

Wild in the Kitchen

Then check your cupboard for any of these items and add some of them to the pot:

¼ cup orzo or other small pasta
¼ cup red or green lentils, rinsed
a handful of sun-dried tomatoes
1 teaspoon of any of the following dried (or fresh) herbs, in combination:
*   parsley, basil, dill, chives, or whatever else you want to use*

Let the soup simmer for about half an hour, or until the orzo, pasta, or lentils are cooked. Season with salt and pepper to taste, and serve. If you have Parmesan cheese, sprinkle some on top. If you have croutons, throw a few on top of the soup, too. Serves 4–6.

Field Notes

Mushrooms

Morels, Chanterelles, and Puffballs

For many, mushrooms are the food of the gods! You'll find them everywhere in the woods and sometimes even growing on your front lawn. Some are edible, others are highly poisonous. The trick is how to tell the difference, and for this you should buy a good guide book and study the examples illustrated very carefully. Even better, find an expert mycologist and have him or her take you on a trip into the woods.

Morels are difficult to find and for this reason, most cherished. (They are also my favorite!) Once you find a spot bearing this treasure, you may want to keep this a deep, dark secret, revealed to no one. Morels have hollow stems and their tops look spongelike, gray or yellowish in color. But there are false morels, too. These are brown or crimson and look brainlike. Don't pick these as they are somewhat toxic.

Chanterelles are a golden yellow color with hollow stems and a funnel shape. Try to find them in their early stages because that's when they're the tastiest. (They have a smell similar to apricots.) Just don't get fooled and pick a false chanterelle.

Puffballs emerge just before autumn and can grow as large as a soccer ball (which they resemble as well). They should be eaten when fresh and bright white. Just peel, slice, and fry in butter for a really tasty treat.

Other wild mushrooms that I like are shaggy manes, boletes, and hen of the woods. But there are many more out there that you might have an easier time finding in your particular area.

One overall rule to keep in mind when you become a mushroom maniac: Never eat a raw mushroom, even if you're sure it isn't poisonous. And always be careful out there!

chanterelles

A Word about Drying Mushrooms

The flavor of wild mushrooms intensifies if you use them dried and reconstitute them in boiling water (for 20 minutes, or until soft). Then you have not only lovely moist mushrooms, but also a delicious liquid that can be used in many recipes as a soup base or stock.

A food dehydrator is perfect for drying mushrooms. If you don't have one, place the mushrooms on a cookie sheet lined with parchment paper. Turn the oven on its lowest setting (150°F) and check after 10–12 hours. The mushrooms should be dry but not really blackened. I once let my mushrooms dry overnight, checking them in the morning. Even at a low oven setting, the darn things went black on me. I was upset, thinking they were spoiled, but tried reconstituting them anyhow. They made a dark, rich broth and did not have a burnt taste.

I noticed, however, that when I used the food dehydrator, the mushrooms were not as black and stayed larger (when dried) than when I tried the same thing in the conventional oven. If you find a large cache of morels, chanterelles, or any other mushroom, a dehydrator is a wise investment.

A really economical way to dry mushrooms is to string them together on a long cord. Just thread a darning needle with cotton thread (or even unflavored dental floss or fishing line), pierce each mushroom, and string it onto your line, until your mushroom garland is as long as you like. Hang from an arch or overhang, so your mushroom garland can float freely and air dry. It also makes a nice decoration in the kitchen . . . and a real conversation piece.

morels

Cream of Wild Mushroom Soup

2 oz. dried wild mushrooms (morels, hen of the woods, chanterelles, etc.)
3 tablespoons butter
1 medium onion, chopped
1 garlic clove, finely chopped
4 tablespoons milk
grated nutmeg (to taste)
3 tablespoons butter
⅓ cup flour
¼–½ cup milk
salt and pepper to taste

Reconstitute mushrooms by boiling in 3½–4 cups water for 20–30 minutes or until soft. Drain mushrooms, reserving the broth, and chop them.

Heat 3 tablespoons butter with the onion and garlic and sauté for 3 minutes. Add the reconstituted wild mushrooms and sauté for 5 more minutes. Add milk and nutmeg and cook for a few more minutes. Set aside.

In another saucepan, melt 3 tablespoons of butter. Remove pan from heat and beat in the flour. Return pan to low heat and cook until mixture turns a darker color. Then remove pan again from heat and add mushroom broth gradually, stirring constantly to avoid lumps. Return to low heat. (If necessary, to get rid of lumps, run the mixture through a sieve, scraping the underside of it to get all the flour mixture.) Then add the cooked mushroom mixture to the broth mixture.

Bring soup to a boil and let it simmer for 20 minutes. Then add ¼–½ cup milk to desired thickness. Heat through and serve. Add salt and pepper to taste. Serves 4.

Wild in the Kitchen

Charred Chicken with Fettucini and Creamed Morels

4 skinless, boneless chicken breasts
   (seasoned with salt, pepper, and lemon juice)
1–2 oz. dried morels
2 cups boiling water
12 oz. spinach fettucini
1 cup white wine
1 cup heavy cream
2 teaspoons fresh dill weed, chopped

¼ cup butter
½ cup flour
1½ cups milk
1 cup scallions, sliced
   (green and white parts)
2 teaspoons fresh lemon juice
salt and pepper (to taste)

Prepare chicken breasts and grill them (or you may broil them in the oven) until slightly blackened and charred and no longer pink inside. Set aside to cool (can be done a day ahead) and serve at room temperature.

Put morels in heat-proof dish and pour 2 cups boiling water on them (to reconstitute). Set aside for 20 minutes or until softened. Remove mushrooms from liquid (reserve liquid for later). Chop mushrooms coarsely.

Cook fettucini according to package directions. Drain and keep warm.

Put mushrooms and wine in a skillet. Bring it to a boil for about 3 minutes, until wine is reduced somewhat. Turn heat to low, then add the cream and dill. Cook on low one more minute. Add reserved mushroom liquid. Cook for 10 minutes.

Meanwhile melt butter in a small saucepan. Add flour and cook for a few minutes over medium heat until mixture has darkened a bit. Slowly add milk, whisking it so there are no lumps. Cook for 5 minutes. Then add this mixture to the mushrooms. Add scallions, lemon juice, salt, and pepper and heat through.

Divide pasta among four plates. Pour morel sauce on the pasta. Slice charred chicken on the diagonal and place on top of pasta. Drizzle a little more sauce on top of the chicken. Serves 4.

Morel Pizza

1 10-inch pizza shell, prebaked
1 tablespoon olive oil
8–10 fresh basil leaves
10 or more fresh morels, depending on their size
¼ cup crumbled feta cheese
¾ cup shredded mozzarella cheese
salt and pepper

Preheat oven to 425°F. Brush pizza shell with 1 tablespoon of olive oil. Cut the basil leaves coarsely and place them on the pizza shell. Wash morels thoroughly, slice them vertically through the middle (checking for critters), and pat them dry with a paper towel. Then, arrange morels cut side down on the pizza. Sprinkle with crumbled feta, then shredded mozzarella. Add salt and pepper. Bake for 10–15 minutes or until the mozzarella is melted.

Serves 2–3 people, depending on appetites.

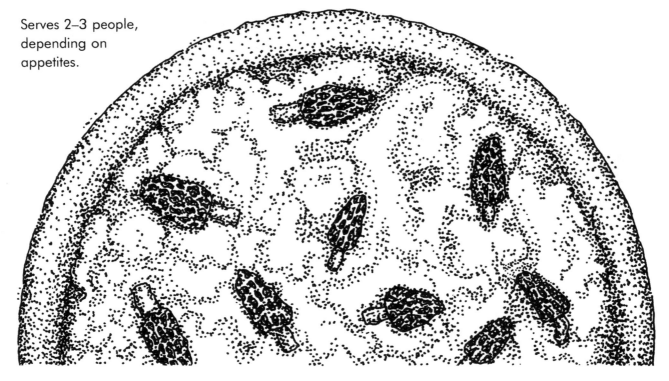

Wild in the Kitchen

Pan-Fried Morels

If you have just returned from the woods with a bag full of morels and are anxious to taste them, this might be the quickest way to enjoy your bounty. Just wash them carefully, making sure you get all the dirt out of the crevices on the caps. Then slice them vertically and look for any ants that might have made the morels their home. Put the morels in a colander or lay them on paper towels to dry.

3 tablespoons butter
10–20 or more morels, depending on their size
salt and freshly ground pepper

Melt the butter in (preferably) a cast iron skillet (if you use a nonstick frying pan, the mushrooms will not brown as nicely). Add halved mushrooms and let fry until their edges start to brown, 5–10 minutes. (Depending on how fresh your morels are, they might contain a lot of water; therefore, it might be necessary to drain a bit of this off while frying.) They are ready when they start to "dance." When the morels start to hop up and down, you'll know it is the right time to eat them. Add salt and pepper and serve hot.

Remember: the mushrooms shrink in size, so 40 mushroom halves (20 mushrooms) do not go a long way. But they are delicious, so savor every bite!

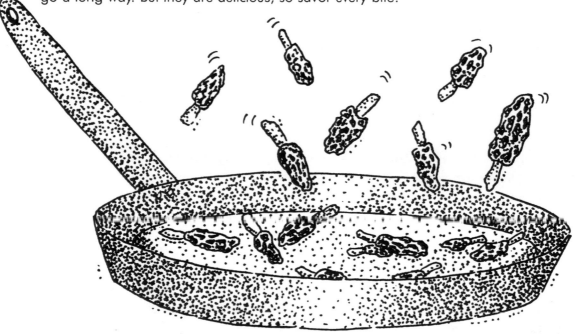

Mushrooms

Wild Mushroom and Asparagus Strudel

2 oz. dried wild mushrooms (morels, hen of the woods, chanterelles, etc.)
2 cups boiling water
½ pound fresh asparagus
4 oz. package (or 125 g) goat cheese
4 oz. package (or 125 g) cream cheese (regular or light)
1 tablespoon fresh chives, chopped
1 tablespoon fresh parsley, chopped
¼ teaspoon salt
¼ teaspoon ground black pepper
10 sheets phyllo dough, defrosted
⅓ cup butter, melted

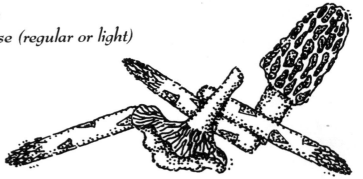

Reconstitute dried mushrooms in 2 cups of boiling water. Set aside for 15 minutes. Strain off liquid (freeze for future use) and drain the mushrooms very, very well. Set the mushrooms on a few tea towels and press lightly to get out all the liquid.

Clean asparagus and snap off tough bases. Cut the spears into 1-inch pieces and set in a pan of water on the stove. Bring to a boil and cook for 5 minutes. Drain and rinse under cold water. Set aside on tea towels and dry the asparagus very well.

Combine the cheeses with the chives, parsley, salt, and pepper and mix well. Stir in the mushrooms and asparagus.

Place a sheet of phyllo dough horizontally in front of you and brush with a little melted butter. Repeat this process until you have 5 stacked sheets of phyllo. Don't brush the top one with butter. Take half the cheese filling and spread it in a 4-inch strip along the bottom of the phyllo (about 1 inch from the bottom and 2 inches from the sides). Fold up the bottom and tuck in the sides and roll it up just like a jelly roll. Put it on a greased cookie sheet, seam side down. Brush all over with melted butter. Cut several small slits along the top of the strudel. Make another strudel by repeating the above process with the other half of the filling.

Bake in a 375°F oven for 30–40 minutes or until golden brown. Before cutting into slices (a serrated or bread knife works best) and serving, let it cool for about a quarter hour or so. Makes 2 strudels, which serve about 6–8 people.

Field Notes

Field Notes

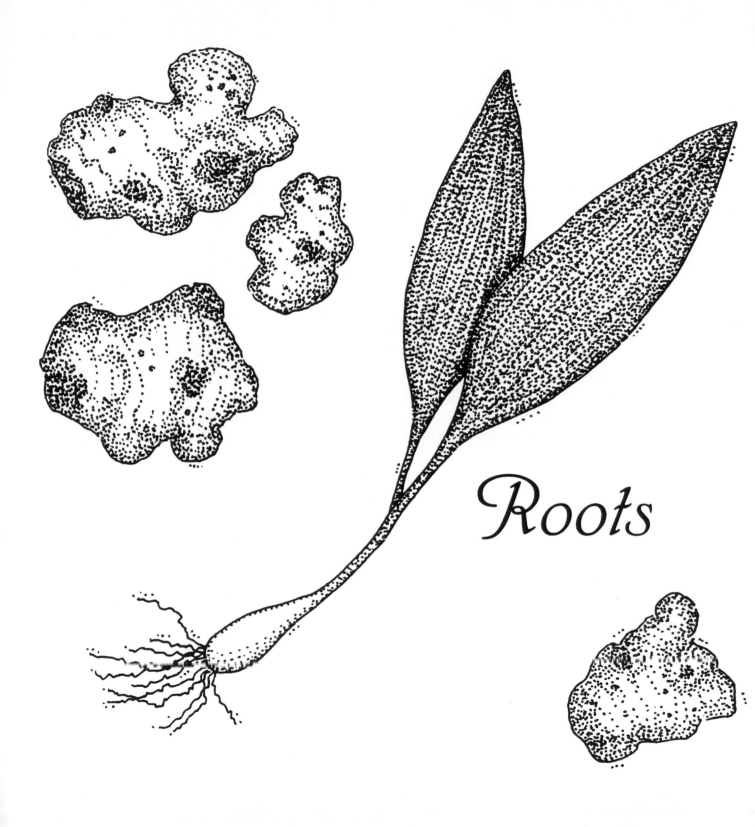

Roots

Ginger

In springtime, one of the first plants to appear in the woods is wild ginger. It has 2 large heart-shaped leaves that sit on hairy stems. And it sports a lovely maroon flower, which rests on the ground and is very easy to miss.

Wild ginger is much more subtle in flavor than store-bought tropical ginger root. But our native wild ginger has a wonderfully earthy taste and is worth seeking out. Its long roots grow horizontally and not very deep in the ground, so they are easy to dig up. Choose a healthy-looking group of wild ginger and don't dig it all up. Since you destroy the plant when you dig up its roots, it's nice to leave some in the ground for next year.

To clean, remove the small, hairy roots that grow off the main one, then wash the root very well in running water. I find it best to run a paring knife over the root to remove its fine membrane. This reveals yellowish-white flesh that darkens (like an apple) when exposed to air.

Wild in the Kitchen

Wild Ginger Tea

3 roots (about 2 to 3 inches in length), chopped into ½-inch pieces
2 cups of water

Add the scrubbed roots to a small pot of water. Bring to a boil and cover; then turn down heat and let simmer for 10 minutes. Strain into a mug. Delicious served with a spoonful of honey, and very soothing for an upset tummy.

You may also dry the roots, after cleaning them. Set them on a baking sheet and put into a 200°F oven for 3–4 hours. Dried wild ginger roots can be stored indefinitely in an airtight jar. These can be used for making wild ginger tea all winter long.

Wild Ginger Pound Cake

Although fresh wild ginger is the main flavor of this cake, it is nudged along by the addition of dry, ground, commercially packaged ginger. This helps intensify its ginger taste.

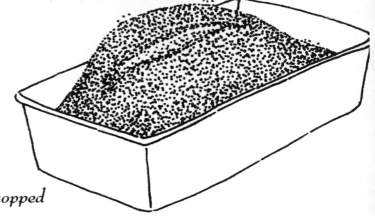

2¼ cups flour
1 teaspoon baking powder
1 teaspoon salt
1 teaspoon ground ginger
⅔ cup butter, softened
1 cup sugar
3 eggs
2 tablespoons fresh wild ginger root, chopped
½ teaspoon vanilla
½ cup milk

Glaze:

2 1-oz. squares of semisweet baking chocolate or ½ cup semisweet chocolate morsels
1 tablespoon butter

In a medium bowl combine flour, baking powder, salt, and ground ginger. Set aside.

In a mixing bowl cream the butter and sugar until light and fluffy. Add the eggs, one at a time, beating well after each addition.

Meanwhile, in a food processor fitted with a metal blade, grind the peeled wild ginger root until pulverized. Add it to the egg mixture, along with the vanilla, and beat well. Then add the dry ingredients a little at a time, alternating with the milk. Beat well.

Spoon the batter into a well-greased 5 × 9-inch loaf pan. Bake at 325°F for 1 hour and 10 minutes. Wait at least 10 minutes before removing the cake from its pan, then cool completely before glazing.

To glaze: Over low heat, melt the chocolate and butter in a small saucepan, stirring until smooth. Drizzle over loaf and let cool before serving.

Wild in the Kitchen

Jerusalem Artichokes

The Jerusalem artichoke never saw the Holy Land! The origin of its name apparently stems from a confusion of descriptive Italian, Spanish, and Arabic languages.

This much-cultivated native has been recorded and known to the North American habitat since the 1600s. It is an edible tuber from a sunflower plant that grows up to 6 feet tall but has a rather small bloom. Raw, it tastes like a water chestnut. Cooked, it tastes like a nutty, sweetish potato. So it can be baked and used as a potato substitute, or julienned and served as a dipping veggie.

The Jerusalem artichoke blooms in late summer; one plant can yield dozens of underground treasures. If you decide to plant them close to home, be careful where you put them, as they are hard to eradicate.

Jerusalem Artichoke Fritters

4 cups Jerusalem artichokes, shredded
1 small onion, grated
3 eggs
1 teaspoon salt
¼ teaspoon pepper
¼ cup flour
2 teaspoons baking powder
vegetable oil for frying

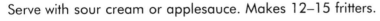

Peel the artichokes and shred in a food processor (or by hand) and put in a mixing bowl. Finely grate a small onion (I usually do this by hand, as I find the food processor makes the onion too mushy) and add into bowl. Blend in eggs, salt, pepper, flour, and baking powder. Mix thoroughly.

In a frying pan, heat a few tablespoons of vegetable oil on medium-high heat. Put a large spoonful of the artichoke mixture into the frying pan. Add as many as will fit in your pan and fry until brown around the edges (3–5 minutes). Then turn over and cook another 3–5 minutes, until golden and crispy. Turn fritters onto a plate covered with paper towels, to blot off excess oil. Keep warm in the oven. Add more oil to the frying pan (as needed) and repeat above procedure with the fritter batter.

Serve with sour cream or applesauce. Makes 12–15 fritters.

Hot Pickled Jerusalem Artichokes

This recipe is based on an old Pennsylvania Dutch recipe. But because these pickles are unusual, your friends will think you are letting them try something totally new.

1½ to 2 pounds Jerusalem artichokes
3 cups white vinegar
¼ cup honey
2 teaspoons turmeric
5 dried red hot peppers
5 cloves garlic
25 peppercorns
10 whole cloves
5 bay leaves
2½ teaspoons mustard seed

Wash the artichokes very well, removing all dirt (if they are scrubbed very well, they needn't be peeled). Slice them into quarter-inch pieces. Set aside. Work quickly, as sliced Jerusalem artichokes will start to discolor once they are exposed to air. Or set them in a bowl of water with a dash of lemon juice to prevent discoloration until ready to use.

In a stainless steel or porcelain-coated saucepan, bring vinegar, honey, and turmeric to a simmer. Meanwhile, sterilize 5 pint jars. In each jar place a dried pepper, a clove of garlic, 5 peppercorns, 2 whole cloves, a bay leaf, and ½ teaspoon of mustard seed. Then add the sliced Jerusalem artichokes to the jars, packing them tightly. Fill each jar with the simmering liquid and seal. Process in a hot water bath (see pages 14–15 for instructions). Yields: 5 pint (500 mL) jars.

Jerusalem Artichoke Soup

2 tablespoons butter
2 medium onions, chopped
2 stalks of celery with leaves, chopped
3–4 large carrots, chopped
1 teaspoon ground ginger
1 pound Jerusalem artichokes, scrubbed or peeled
4 cups chicken (or vegetable) broth
salt and pepper to taste
½ cup sour cream (or plain yogurt)
mint leaves (optional)

Melt butter in a large pot. Add the onions, celery, carrots, and ginger. Soften the vegetables over medium-low heat for about 5 minutes.

Cut scrubbed (or peeled) artichokes into chunks. Add them to the pot along with the broth. Cover and let simmer for 15–20 minutes or until the artichokes are soft. Let cool. Purée all ingredients in a food processor or blender. Put contents through a fine sieve. (If you have peeled the artichokes beforehand, you might not find this step necessary.)

Return mixture to the pot and reheat. Season with salt and pepper. Ladle soup into bowls and top each with a dollop of sour cream (or plain yogurt). Garnish with mint leaves. Makes 4 servings.

Wild Leeks

Wild leek (also known as wild onion, wild garlic, or ramps) belongs to the lily family. When the leaves are very young and tender, they can be added to a tossed salad. As soon as its broad, tapered leaves have come out fully, dig the wild leek up and make sure to keep the roots attached and dirty until you're ready to use them. If you wash wild leek clean and keep it for hours, it'll soon lose its freshness.

Wild leek has a very delicate flavor when cooked. Some people love to eat it raw. Careful . . . there may be social repercussions.

And remember, because you are digging the roots, you are essentially killing the plant. So a general rule of thumb is to always leave more than you take. The best part about that is you'll have some for next year and the year after that (provided you keep your spot a well-guarded secret).

Creamy Wild Leek Salad Dressing

5–6 wild leeks, white part only
½ teaspoon dry mustard
½ teaspoon salt
¼ teaspoon freshly ground pepper
1 teaspoon sugar
juice of ½ a lemon
2 tablespoons white vinegar
6 tablespoons olive oil

Put all ingredients in a food processor or blender and process until smooth and creamy. Will keep for a week in the refrigerator.

Serving suggestion: Pour salad dressing over romaine lettuce with slices of hard-boiled egg and crumbled bacon.

Wild in the Kitchen

Roasted Wild Leek and Potatoes

5–6 medium potatoes
30 wild leeks, white part only
2–3 tablespoons oil
¼–½ teaspoon cayenne pepper
salt and pepper to taste

Scrub the potatoes well, leaving the skin on. Cut them into wedges and put into a mixing bowl. Clean the wild leeks very well and cut off the green ends, leaving just the heads, and add them to the bowl. Sprinkle oil, cayenne, salt, and pepper on top and mix well, making sure to coat everything. Put the oil-coated potatoes and leeks onto a foil-lined baking pan. Bake uncovered at 400°F for one hour, or until potatoes have browned. Make sure to stir the potatoes once or twice while cooking, to brown them evenly. Transfer into a bowl or casserole and serve piping hot. Makes enough for 6 people.

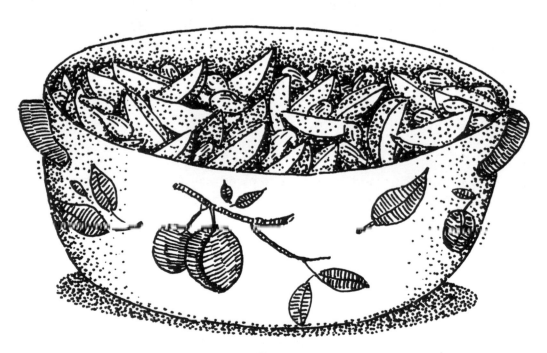

Wild Leek and Potato Soup

Wild leeks become sweet when sautéed. This flavor combines well with the earthy taste of the potatoes. A really delicious spring soup.

2 tablespoons butter
¼ cup water
35–40 wild leeks, white part only
4–5 medium-sized potatoes
5 cups chicken or vegetable
*   stock*
salt and pepper to taste
1–2 wild leek leaves
*   (for garnish)*

Put a large pot over low heat and add the butter and water. When the butter has melted, add the cleaned, chopped leeks. Sauté gently until the leeks get tender, but not brown, about 15 minutes.

Peel the potatoes and chop them coarsely. Add them to the leeks, along with the chicken stock. Bring to a boil, reduce heat, cover the pot, and cook about 30 minutes or until the potatoes are soft.

Put this mixture into a blender or food processor and purée until smooth (you might have to do this in batches). Season with salt and pepper. If the soup is too thick, thin it with a bit more stock or water until it is the desired consistency.

Ladle the soup into bowls and top with a few thinly sliced wild leek leaves. Makes 4–6 servings.

 Field Notes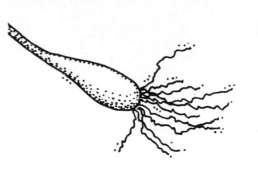

Latin Names

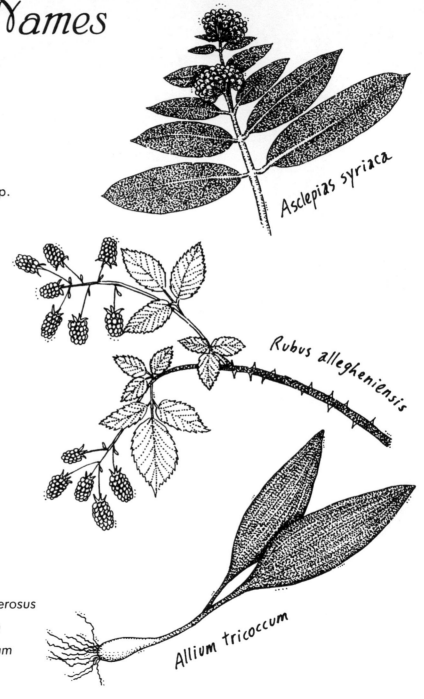

Apple, wild—*Pyrus spp.*

Barberry—*Berberis vulgaris*

Blackberry—*Rubus allegheniensis*

Blueberry, huckleberry—*Vaccinium spp.*

Bolete—*Boletus spp.*

Chanterelle—*Cantharellus cibarius*

Cloudberry—*Rubus chamaemorus*

Clover—*Trifolium spp.*

   Red clover—*Trifolium pratense*

Crabapple—*Pyrus coronaria*

Currant—*Ribes spp.*

Dandelion—*Taraxacum officinale*

Day lily—*Hemerocallis fulva*

Elder—*Sambucus canadensis*

Fiddlehead—*Pteretis pensylvanica*

Ginger—*Asarum canadense*

Gooseberry—*Ribes spp.*

Grape, wild—*Vitis spp.*

Ground cherry—*Physalis spp.*

Hawthorn—*Crataegus spp.*

Hen of the woods—*Grifola frondosa*

Jerusalem artichoke—*Helianthus tuberosus*

Labrador tea—*Ledum groenlandicum*

Lamb's quarters—*Chenopodium album*

Leek, wild—*Allium tricoccum*

Milkweed—*Asclepias syriaca*

Asclepias syriaca

Rubus allegheniensis

Allium tricoccum

Wild in the Kitchen

Mint, wild—*Mentha arvensis*

    Peppermint—*Mentha piperita*

    Spearmint—*Mentha spicata*

Morel—*Morchella esculenta*

Nannyberry—*Viburnum lentago*

Partridgeberry—*Mitchella repens*

Plantain—*Plantago major*

Puffball—*Calvatia gigantea*

Purslane—*Portulaca oleracea*

Raspberry, black—*Rubus occidentalis*

    red—*Rubus idaeus var. strigosus*

Shaggy mane—*Coprinus comatus*

Strawberry, wild—*Fragaria virginiana*

Sumac—*Rhus typhina*

Violet, blue—*Viola papilionacea*

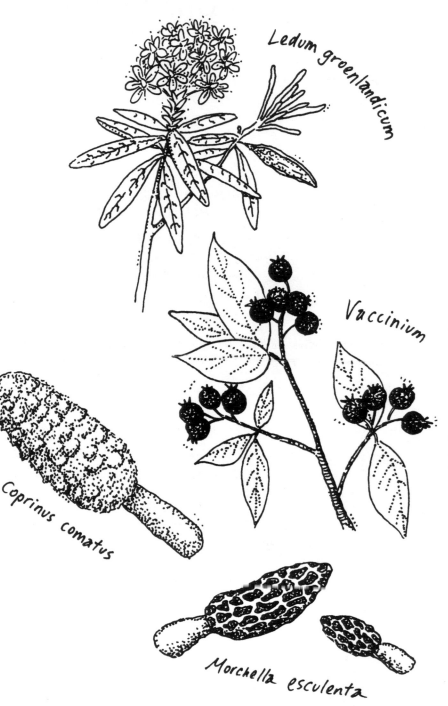

Ledum groenlandicum

Vaccinium

Coprinus comatus

Morchella esculenta

Recommended Reading

I have found all of the following books very useful while gathering information about wild edibles. Some of the books are out of print, but I have been able to locate them in the library or used bookstores. Many online booksellers have out-of-print search services to help you find older books. Or try used-book Web sites, where they might also be available.

Angier, Bradford. *Free for the Eating,* Harrisburg, PA: Stackpole Books, 1971.
    No recipes but good descriptions of wild plants with black-and-white line drawings. Out of print. Look for other books by Bradford Angier, like his Field Guide to Wild Edible Plants, *1974, which is full of color illustrations and available at most bookstores.*

Berglund, Berndt. *Wilderness Survival,* Toronto: Pagurian Press Limited, 1975.

Berglund, Berndt, and Clare E. Bolsby. *The Edible Wild,* Toronto: Pagurian Press Limited, 1974.
    Both of these books by Berndt Berglund are out of print but well worth searching out. They are full of survival information and have very interesting recipes (especially for those who get lost in the woods for a week or so).

Boorman, Sylvia. *Wild Plums in Brandy,* Toronto: McGraw Hill Company, 1962.
    A charming book illustrated with lovely woodcuts. Unfortunately it is out of print.

Buszek, Beatrice Ross. *The Blueberry Connection,* Granville Centre, Nova Scotia: Cranberrie Cottage, 1990.
    One hundred things to do with a blueberry. Handwritten and very homey. Useful, out of print.

Carson, Dale. *New Native American Cooking,* New York: Random House, Inc., 1996.
    From frogs legs to succotash. Native American recipes for the modern kitchen with historical descriptions and folklore.

Duff, Gail. *The Country-Side Cook Book,* New York: Van Nostrand Reinhold Company, 1982.
    Beautifully illustrated in color, this book includes recipes for the table as well as the medicine chest. Out of print.

Duff, Gail. *The Fruit & Nut Book,* London: Sidgwick & Jackson, 1990.
    A terrific book, chock-a-block full of recipes for every fruit and nut you can think of, and many you never heard of, too. Out of print.

Elias, Thomas S., and Peter A. Dykeman. *Edible Wild Plants: A North American Field Guide,* New York: Sterling Publishing Co. Inc., 1990.
    A must for identification, this book has detailed color photos of wild edibles.

Gardon, Anne. *The Wild Food Gourmet*, Willowdale, Ontario: Firefly Books Ltd., 1998.
A lovely cookbook with beautiful photographs, it is more of a gourmet cookbook and not a survival one. A feast for the eyes, as well as the stomach.

Garrett, Blanche Pownall. *Canadian Country Preserves & Wines*, Toronto: James Lewis & Samuel, 1974.

Garrett, Blanche Pownall. *A Taste of the Wild*, Toronto: James Lorimer & Company, 1975.
Both of these books by Blanche Pownall Garrett are out of print, but I highly recommend them. There are some lovely stories describing foraging outings. The recipes are fairly simple and interesting.

George, Jean Craighead. *Acorn Pancakes, Dandelion Salad and 38 Other Wild Recipes*, New York: HarperCollins, 1995.
Good book for introducing children to the edible wild. All the wild plants are very simple to find and identify. Nice color drawings and recipes that are aimed at kids.

Gibbons, Euell. *Stalking the Wild Asparagus*, reprint ed., New York: Alan C. Hood & Co., 1987.
The book that basically started it all! A really good, interesting read, and some good recipes, too.

Grieve, Mrs. M. *A Modern Herbal*, New York: Dover Publications Inc., 1978.
Everything you wanted to know about herbs . . . and I mean it! Heavy duty, encyclopedic-type book. A reprint that was originally published in 1931.

Harris, Ben Charles. *Eat the Weeds*, Barre, MA: Barre Publishers, 1971.
Out of print but worth looking for. Good basic wild edible book with recipes and historical backgrounds.

Henderson, Robert K. *The Neighborhood Forager*, White River Junction, VT: Chelsea Green Publishing Co., 2000.
Interesting book with lots of historical and medicinal uses for things found in your backyard.

Jordan, Peter. *The New Guide to Mushrooms*, London: Anness Publishing Limited, 1998.
Coffee-table book with lots of color photographs. Limited number of species cited. This is a good companion book but not recommended as your only sourcebook for mushroom hunting.

Kavasch, E. Barrie. *Guide to Northeastern Wild Edibles*, Surrey, British Columbia: Hancock House, 1981.
Simple identification book with some good photos. Specific species growing in the northeast only. Out of print.

Laessoe, Thomas, Anna Del Conte, and Gary Lincoff. *The Knopf Mushroom Book*, Toronto: Knopf, 1996.
One of the best mushroom identification books. Very large size—it is not a pocket guide—but well worth owning. Full of very descriptive color photos and drawings, a must for mushroom fanatics and beginners, too.

Meuninck, Jim, and Dr. Jim Duke. *Edible Wild Plants* (video). Edwardsburg, MI: Media Methods, 1988.
A good video and fun to watch. Sort of a travelogue with foraging and cooking demonstrations.

Peterson, Lee Allen. *A Field Guide to Edible Wild Plants: Eastern and Central North America*, Boston: Houghton Mifflin Co., 1999.
The best wild edible identification pocket guide with wonderful black-and-white illustrations and some color plates. Take this one with you everywhere you go!

Runyon, Linda. *Lawn Food Cook Book*, Glens Falls, NY: Williams Graphic Arts, 1985.
A small booklet full of informative wild recipes that use no milk, eggs, or cheese. Out of print but look for it at tag sales or flea markets.

Schneider, Elizabeth. *Uncommon Fruits & Vegetables*, New York: Harper & Row, Inc., 1989.
A wonderful book full of fruits and vegetables, wild and otherwise. Very interesting background information and terrific recipes. Nice drawings, too. Out of print.

Szczawinski, Adam F., and Nancy J. Turner. *Edible Garden Weeds of Canada*, Markham, Ontario: Fitzhenry & Whiteside, 1988.
Good book with photos and drawings, identification facts, and recipes. Very useful but out of print.

Tatum, Billy Joe. *Wild Foods Field Guide & Cookbook*, New York: Workman Publishing Company, 1985.
Lots and lots of recipes and descriptions of many wild edibles. A fun book to read.

Turner, Nancy J., and Adam F. Szczawinski. *Edible Wild Fruits and Nuts of Canada*, Markham, Ontario: Fitzhenry & Whiteside, 1988.
Useful, informative, and, sadly, out of print.

Weiner, Michael A. *Earth Medicine—Earth Food: Plant Remedies, Drugs, and Natural Foods of the North American Indians*, New York: Fawcett Books, 1991.
A guide to wild plants used by Native Americans, mostly as cures rather than edibles. Interesting facts and background information, with some illustrations.

Index

Apples:
about, 72
Wild Apple Butter, 74
Wild Apple Chutney, 76
Wild Apple Pudding, 75
Barberries:
about, 18
Barberry Jelly, 19
Barberry Sweet/Savory Syrup, 19
Berries:
Barberries,
about, 18
Barberry Jelly, 19
Barberry Sweet/Savory Syrup,19
Black Raspberries,
about, 42
Marci's Raspberry Chicken, 45
Raspberry Galette, 44
Raspberry Pudding Cake, 43
Raspberry Vinegar, 45
Blackberries,
about, 20
Blackberry Crisp, 22
Tipsy Blackberries, 21
Blueberries,
about, 23
Wild Blueberry Muffin Cake, 25
Wild Blueberry Squares, 24
Wild Blueberry Syrup, 27
Wild Blue Yonder Pudding, 26
Cloudberries,
about, 28
Cloudberry Muffins, 29
Currants,
about, 30
Wild Cassis, 31
Wild Cassis Cocktails, 32
Elderberries,
about, 33
Elderberry Marmalade, 35
Elderberry and Peach cake, 37
Elderberry Triangles, 34
Elderberry Wine, 36
Gooseberries,
about, 30
Nannyberries,
about, 38
Spiced Nannyberry Butter, 41
Partridgeberries,

about, 28
Jam, 28
Raspberries, black,
about, 42
Marci's Raspberry Chicken, 45
Raspberry Galette, 44
Raspberry Pudding Cake, 43
Raspberry Vinegar, 45
Raspberries, red,
about, 42
Marci's Raspberry Chicken, 44
Raspberry Galette, 45
Raspberry Pudding Cake, 43
Raspberry Vinegar, 45
Strawberries,
about, 46
Lemon Tarts with Wild Strawberries, 49
Wild Strawberry Fool, 50
Wild Strawberry Sauce, 47
Wild Strawberry Smoothie, 48
Beverages:
Elderberry Wine, 36
Elderflower Bubbly, 61
A Nice Cup of Labrador Tea, 94
Pink Sumac Lemonade, 63
Sunny Mint Iced Tea, 104
Sumac Spritzer, 63
Wild Cassis, 31
Wild Cassis Cocktails, 32
Wild Ginger Tea, 125
Wild Strawberry Smoothie, 48
Black Raspberries:
about, 42
Marci's Raspberry Chicken, 45
Raspberry Galette, 44
Raspberry Pudding cake, 43
Raspberry Vinegar, 45
Blackberries:
about, 42
Blackberry Crisp, 22
Tipsy Blackberries, 21
Blueberries:
about, 23
Wild Blueberry Muffin Cake, 25
Wild Blueberry Squares, 24
Wild Blueberry Syrup, 27
Wild Blue Yonder Pudding, 26
Butter:
Wild Apple Butter, 74

Spiced Nannyberry Butter, 41
Cake:
Elderberry and Peach Cake, 37
Raspberry Pudding Cake, 43
Wild Blueberry Muffin Cake, 25
Wild Ginger Pound Cake, 126
Canada Moonseed, 77
Candied Violets, 65
Canning rules, 14-15
Cassis, Wild, 31
Chanterelles, 114
Chicken:
Charred Chicken with Fettuccini and
Creamed Morels, 117
Marci's Raspberry Chicken, 45
Chokecherries:
about, 68
Chokecherry Marmalade, 71
Chokecherry and Pecan Conserve, 69
Hot! Hot! Hot! Chokecherry Chutney, 70
Chutney:
definition, 15
Hot! Hot! Hot! Chokecherry Chutney, 70
Wild Apple Chutney, 76
Cloudberries:
about, 28
Cloudberry Muffins, 29
Clover:
about, 54
Clover Blossom Vinegar, 55
Pink Clover Vinaigrette, 55
Cocktails, 32
Conserve:
Chokecherry and Pecan Conserve, 69
definition, 15
Crabapples:
about, 72
Spiced Crabapples, 73
Crisp:
Blackberry Crisp, 22
Currants:
about, 30
Wild Cassis, 31
Wild Cassis Cocktails, 32
Dandelions:
about, 84
Braised Dandelion Greens with Blue
Cheese and Almonds, 85
Dandelion Flower Marmalade Jelly, 56

Wilted Dandelion Salad, 86
Day Lilies:
  about, 57
  Sautéed Day Lilly Buds, 59
  Spicy Ginger Day Lily Buds, 58
  Steamed Day Lily Buds, 59
  Stuffed Day Lily Blossoms, 60
Elderberries:
  about, 33
  Elderberry Marmalade, 35
  Elderberry and Peach Cake, 37
  Elderberry Triangles, 34
  Elderberry Wine, 36
Elderflowers:
  about, 33
  Elderflower Bubbly, 61
False morels, 114
Fiddleheads:
  about, 87
  Cream of Fiddlehead Soup, 90
  Fiddlehead Pickles, 88
  Sautéed Fiddleheads, 89
Flowers:
  Clover,
    about, 54
  Clover Blossom Vinegar, 55
    Pink Clover Vinaigrette, 55
  Dandelion Flowers,
    about , 84
    Dandelion Flower Marmalade Jelly, 56
  Day Lilies,
    about, 57
    Sautéed Day Lily Buds, 59
    Spicy Ginger Day Lily Buds, 58
    Steamed Day Lily Buds, 59
    Stuffed Day Lily Blossoms, 60
  Sumac,
    about, 62
    Pink Sumac Lemonade, 63
    Sumac Spritzer, 63
  Violets,
    about, 64
    Candied Violets, 65
Fool, Wild Strawberries, 50
Fruit Butter:
  definition, 15
  Spiced Nannyberry Butter, 41
  Wild Apple Butter, 72
Fruits:
  Apples,
    about, 72
    Wild Apple Butter, 74
    Wild Apple Chutney, 76
    Wild Apple Pudding, 75
  Chokecherries,

about, 68
Hot! Hot! Hot! Chokecherry Chutney, 70
Chokecherry Marmalade, 71
Chokecherry and Pecan Conserve, 69
Crabapples,
  about, 72
  Spiced Crabapples, 73
Grapes,
  about, 77
  Wild Grape Jelly, 78
Ground Cherries,
  about, 79
  Ground Cherry Jelly, 80
Hawthorns,
  about, 39
  Hawthorn Jelly, 40
Galette, Raspberry, 44
Gel testing, 15
Ginger:
  about, 124
  Wild Ginger Pound Cake, 126
  Wild Ginger Tea, 125
Gooseberries:
  about, 30
Grape Leaves:
  about, 77
  Meat-Stuffed Grape Leaves, 91
  Orange-and-Currant-Stuffed Wild Grape Leaves, 92
Grapes:
  about, 77
  Wild Grape Jelly, 78
Greens:
  Dandelions,
    about, 84
    Braised Dandelion Greens with Blue Cheese and Almonds, 85
    Wilted Dandelion Salad, 86
  Fiddleheads,
    about, 87
    Cream of Fiddlehead Soup, 90
    Fiddlehead Pickles, 88
    Sautéed Fiddleheades, 89
  Grape Leaves,
    about, 77
    Meat-Stuffed Wild Grape Leaves, 91
    Orange-and-Currant-Stuffed Wild Grape Leaves, 92
  Labrador Tea,
    about, 93
    A Nice Cup of Labrador Tea, 94
  Lamb's Quarters,
    about, 95
    Lamb's Quarters and Cheese Pie, 96

Lamb's Quarters and Sun-Dried Tomato Pasta, 97
White Bean Soup and Lamb's Quarters, 98
Milkweed,
  about, 99
  Blanching, 99
  Cheesy Milkweed Pod Hors d'Oeuvres, 102
  Chinese-Style Stir-Fried Milkweed, 101
  Milkweed "Broccoli" Salad, 100
Mint,
  about, 103
  Sunny Mint Iced Tea, 104
  Tabouli Salad, 106
  Wild Mint Ice Cubes, 104
  Wild Mint Jelly, 105
  Wild Mint Sauce, 105
Mustard,
  about, 107
  Mustard-Seed-Pod Pickles, 108
Plantain,
  about, 109
  Wild and Crazy Soup, 110
Purslane,
  about, 109
  Wild and Crazy Soup, 110
Ground Cherries:
  about, 79
  Ground Cherry Jelly, 80
Hawthorns:
  about, 39
  Hawthorn Jelly, 40
Jam:
  definition, 15
  Partridgeberry, 28
Jelly:
  Barberry Jelly, 19
  Dandelion Flower Marmalade Jelly, 56
  definition, 15
  Ground Cherry Jelly, 80
  Hawthorn Jelly, 40
  Wild Grape Jelly, 78
  Wild Mint Jelly, 105
Jerusalem artichokes:
  about, 127
  Hot Pickled Jerusalem Artichokes, 129
  Jerusalem Artichoke Fritters, 128
  Jerusalem Artichoke Soup, 130
Labrador Tea:
  about, 93
  A Nice Cup of Labrador Tea, 94
Lamb's Quarters:
  about, 95
  Lamb's Quarters and Cheese Pie, 96

Lamb's Quarters and Sun-Dried Tomato
    Pasta, 97
White Bean Soup and Lamb's Quarters,
    98
Leeks:
    about, 131
    Creamy Wild Leek Salad Dressing, 132
    Roasted Wild Leek and Potatoes, 133
    Wild Leek and Potato Soup, 134
Marmalade:
    Chokecherry Marmalade, 71
    Dandelion Flower Marmalade Jelly, 56
    definition, 15
    Elderberry Marmalade, 35
Milkweed:
    about, 99
    blanching, 99
    Cheesy Milkweed Pod Hors d'Oeuvres,
    102
    Chinese-Style Stir-Fried Milkweed, 101
    Milkweed "Broccoli" Salad, 100
Mint:
    about, 103
    Sunny Mint Iced Tea, 104
    Tabouli Salad, 106
    Wild Mint Ice Cubes, 104
    Wild Mint Jelly, 105
    Wild Mint Sauce, 105
Morels:
    about, 114
    Charred Chicken with Fettuccini and
        Creamed Morels, 117
    Cream of Wild Mushroom Soup, 116
    drying, 115
    Morel Pizza, 118
    Pan-Fried Morels, 119
    Wild Mushroom and Asparagus Strudel,
    120
Muffins:
    Cloudberry Muffins, 29
Mushrooms:
    about, 114
    Chanterelles, 114
    Cream of Wild Mushroom Soup, 116
    drying, 115
    False morels, 114
    Morels,
        about, 114
        Charred Chicken with Fettuccini and
            Creamed Morels, 117
        Pan-fried Morels, 119
        Morel Pizza, 118
        Wild Mushroom and Asparagus
            Strudel, 120
    Puffballs, 114

Mustard:
    about, 107
    Mustard Seed Pod-Pickles, 108
Nannyberries:
    about, 38
    Spiced Nannyberry Butter, 41
Partridgeberries:
    about, 28
    Jam, 28
Pasta:
    Lamb's Quarters and Sun-Dried Tomato
        Pasta, 97
Pastry:
    Elderberry Triangles, 34
    Lamb's Quarters and Cheese Pie, 96
    Lemon Tarts with Wild Strawberries, 49
    Raspberry Galette, 44
    Wild Mushroom and Asparagus Strudel,
    120
Pickles:
    Fiddlehead Pickles, 88
    Hot Pickled Jerusalem Artichokes, 129
    Mustard Seed Pod Pickles, 108
    Spicy Ginger Day Lily Buds, 58
Pizza, Morel, 118
Plantain:
    about, 109
    Wild and Crazy Soup, 110
Preserve:
    definition, 15
    Preserving Rules, 14
Pudding:
    Wild Apple Pudding, 75
    Wild Blue Yonder Pudding, 26
Puffballs, 114
Purslane:
    about, 109
    Wild and Crazy Soup, 110
Raspberries
    about, 42
    Marci's Raspberry Chicken, 45
    Raspberry Galette, 44
    Raspberry Pudding Cake, 43
    Raspberry Vinegar, 45
Roots:
    Ginger,
        about, 124
        Wild Ginger Pound Cake, 126
        Wild Ginger Tea, 125
    Jerusalem Artichokes,
        about, 127
        Hot Pickled Jerusalem Artichokes, 129
        Jerusalem Artichoke Fritters, 128
        Jerusalem Artichoke Soup, 130
    Leeks,

about, 131
    Creamy Wild Leek Salad Dressing,
    132
    Roasted Wild Leek and Potatoes, 133
    Wild Leek and Potato Soup, 134
Rules for preserving, 14
Salad:
    Milkweed "Broccoli" Salad, 100
    Tabouli Salad, 106
    Wilted Dandelion Salad, 86
Salad dressing:
    Creamy Wild Leek Salad Dressing, 132
    Pink Clover Vinaigrette, 55
Sauce:
    Wild Mint Sauce, 105
    Wild Strawberry Sauce, 47
Smoothie, Wild Strawberry, 48
Soup:
    Cream of Fiddlehead Soup, 90
    Cream of Wild Mushroom Soup, 116
    Jerusalem Artichoke Soup, 130
    White Bean and Lamb's Quarters Soup,
    98
    Wild Leek and Potato Soup, 134
    Wild and Crazy Soup, 110
Squares:
    Wild Blueberry Squares, 24
Strawberries:
    about, 46
    Wild Strawberry Fool, 50
    Lemon Tarts with Wild Strawberries, 49
    Wild Strawberry Sauce, 47
    Wild Strawberry Smoothie, 48
Stuffed grape leaves:
    Meat-Stuffed Wild Grape Leaves, 91
    Orange-and-Currant-Stuffed Wild Grape
        Leaves, 92
Sumac:
    about, 62
    Pink Sumac Lemonade, 63
    Sumac Spritzer, 63
Syrup:
    Barberry Sweet/Savory Syrup, 19
    Wild Blueberry Syrup, 27
Testing for gel point, 15
Vinegar:
    Clover Blossom Vinegar, 45
    Raspberry Vinegar, 45
Violets:
    about, 64
    Candied Violets, 65
Wine, Elderberry, 36

About the Author

Ronna Mogelon is a graphic designer, chef, and amateur naturalist who lives on a farmstead in rural Ontario, Canada. She has a Bachelor of Fine Arts degree from Concordia University in Montreal and studied cooking at George Brown College, Toronto. She became interested in wild edible plants when she moved from Toronto to the country and began to explore the woodlands and meadows that surrounded her farm. Her cooking expertise includes a stint as a prop cake baker and food stylist for the television and movie industry—among her film credits are the cakes and food props for *The Mia Farrow Story*, *Forever Plaid*, *Kung Fu*, and *The Big Comfy Couch*. She has also baked birthday cakes for Mick Jagger and Lauren Hutton.

She is the author of *Famous People's Cats,* a book of cartoons. Currently, she is foraging for a sequel to *Wild in the Kitchen*. She is also involved in video production in Montreal, Toronto, and New York.